LES PARSONS

WRITING IN THE REAL CLASSROOM

HEINEMANN
Portsmouth, NH

© 1991 Pembroke Publishers Limited
528 Hood Road
Markham, Ontario
L3R 3K9

Published in the U.S.A. by
Heinemann Educational Books, Inc.
361 Hanover Street
Portsmouth, NH 03801-3959
ISBN (U.S.) 0-435-08587-5

Library of Congress Cataloging-in-Publication Data

Parsons, Les, 1943-
    Writing in the real classroom / Les Parsons.
        p.   cm.
    Includes bibliographical references.
    ISBN 0-435-08587-5
    1. English-language — Composition and exercises — Study and
teaching. 2. Creative writing — Study and teaching. I. Title.
LB1576.P265 1991
808'.04 — dc20   90-28694
                                         CIP

Canadian Cataloguing in Publication Data

Parsons, Les, 1943-
    Writing in the real classroom
Includes bibliographical references and index.
ISBN 0-921217-61-7

1. Creative writing - Study and teaching (Secondary).
2. Creative writing - Study and teaching
(Elementary). 3. Classroom management. I. Title.
LB1576.P37 1991   808'.042   C91-093275-1

Editor: Art Hughes
Design: John Zehethofer
Cover Photography: Ajay Photographics
Typesetting: Jay Tee Graphics Ltd.

Printed and bound in Canada
9 8 7 6 5 4 3 2 1

Contents

Foreword

In recent years, classroom writing programs have begun to change dramatically. Citing the current focus on the writing process, teachers are re-examining and adjusting their traditional approaches. Unfortunately, a gap has developed between what teachers originally hoped to gain from the writing process and what they actually realized from the myriad, hybrid practices that eventually evolved in classrooms. Acknowledging that the inherent structure of a typical school environment makes it difficult to implement a true writing process, *Writing in the Real Classroom* moves on to show teachers how to accommodate that structure and still revitalize their approach to writing.

As well as offering suggestions to help students develop as independent writers, this comprehensive handbook describes how to use writing as a multi-faceted, learning/teaching tool and not just as a means of communication. Annotated samples of student writing illustrate the various techniques. Specific directions for setting up and marking a writing folder, developing editing and revising procedures, and guiding students in how to conduct peer-revision conferences are also included. From ready-to-use sheets for evaluating narrative and expository writing to a unique, four-stage process for evaluating poetry, *Writing in the Real Classroom: Responding to the Writing Process* offers teachers a wealth of practical resources to help them reassess and refine their writing programs.

1 * A writing classroom in action

Snapshots - past and present

Snapshots — past and present

From the past . . .

Close your eyes and imagine the ideal writing classroom. Are you picturing rows of students, possibly in uniform, heads bent, intently filling page after page in their composition notebooks? Is the teacher moving slowly up and down the aisles, carefully monitoring their efforts, stopping here to encourage one student, there to point out a misspelled word, and always speaking in hushed tones? Is the atmosphere in the classroom reverential, studious, and silent? If so, blink twice and be prepared for a shock.

To the present . . .

In this writing process classroom, you're immediately aware of two unexpected impressions: everyone isn't quiet and everyone isn't writing. Students seem to be everywhere, at informally-grouped desks, on the floor, at computer consoles, or moving casually from one point to another. While some are involved in discussions in pairs or small groups, others are quietly reading novels, magazines, newspapers, or each other's stories, essays, or poems. And some are writing alone, oblivious to whatever is happening around them. At first glance, the range of activities, the constant movement, and the underlying hum of voices seem haphazard, even unsettling. Gradually, however, impressions become more fixed and patterns begin to emerge . . . .

Two students over by the window are engaged in a revision conference. The student author has just finished reading aloud a third draft of her narrative about skate-boarding. Her conference partner begins by saying, "The part about coming down the 'chute' was really exciting, you know, the spot where you said it felt like you had 'a fist stuck down your throat'? That was great! I see why you're worried about the ending, though. Why don't you end it when she crosses the finish line and cut out all the rest? That's where it ended for me anyway . . . . ''

Another student passes in front of them, stops at the shelf where the paper is stored, and picks up some lined refill paper.

Over in the corner, two students are sprawled side by side on a big, red cushion. One is reading "The Homecoming" by Cynthia Voigt; the other is flipping through a Roald Dahl novel. Both are so engrossed that they hardly notice a third student pass by, gingerly stepping over their legs, heading for the writer's supply table to get a stapler and some transparent tape . . . .

Four students are grouped at some desks, holding an impromptu discussion on censorship. They had been astonished to hear earlier in the period that some of the books by a well-known author of young-adult fiction had been banned from some school libraries. The author was scheduled to visit their school the following week. One of the students asks, "Why shouldn't books be censored like the movies? Adults could rate books the way they do movies and kids wouldn't be able to read any stuff that might be bad for them.''

"Sure," replies another, "but who decides what's bad? Besides, if it could hurt kids, wouldn't it hurt the adults who are reading the same things?''

Behind them, a student who had picked up a thesaurus from the writing resource table stops to listen for a moment and then moves on.

A student at the computer is fiddling with the format of a poem she had composed about best friends. Since the poem had no rhyme or rhythm pattern, she wasn't sure where the lines should end. The poem was finished, but she kept rearranging phrases and words, searching for the most satisfying combination . . . .

Beside her, two friends are thumbing through a book rack, commenting on titles they know or have heard about from others.

Nearby, two other students are conducting an editing conference. The author of the piece on pollution asks, "Should it be 'they're' or 'their' in the second sentence?''

The other replies, "I think it's 'their'. But, shouldn't you have a question mark after you say, 'What are their reasons for cutting down the rain forests?' ''

Finally, you spot the teacher sitting in a student's chair, hunched over, eyes closed, listening to a student read a complex narrative about an afterlife and a parallel existence. When the student finishes, the teacher says nothing for a moment.

"Hmm," he eventually mutters, "that description of the old man's death made a lot of connections in my head. It was truly moving. But, somehow, I got disengaged at that point and had a hard time focusing on what followed. What did you especially want to get across to people after that point?"

And so it goes in a writing process classroom. To be totally fair to a typical classroom environment, however, a few more snapshots need to be added . . . .

The principal makes a brief, unexpected announcement over the intercom, two students start to argue over the ownership of a pen, the teacher collects money for a school fund-raiser, a group of students admire someone's new pair of running shoes, two students discuss an upcoming competition in which their dance club is entered, the office signals for the caretaker, again over the intercom, six members of the band are called down for an early lunch before leaving for a special performance at another school, the vice-principal wants to see three students about some graffiti found in one of the washrooms, and the teacher sits with another student talking quietly about an upsetting situation the student is experiencing at home . . . .

These scenes and more are played over and over in every classroom and in every school. Variations occur across the curriculum at every grade level. Thirty or more students from different backgrounds, with different interests, abilities, and personal concerns, and at different stages of physical, emotional, and intellectual development are brought together in one classroom. Add to these variables the unwieldy and intrusive functioning of school administration and the recursive, individual, and unpredictable nature of the writing process itself, and some measure of the complexities involved in writing within the confines of a classroom become apparent.

If teachers were directly responsible for motivating, directing, tracking, and evaluating the writing development of each individual student, the dimensions of the task would be boundless and the load would be overwhelming. Fortunately, teachers can take advantage of the fact that writing must necessarily become the responsibility of the writer and that writing and learning go hand in hand. By devising stimulating questions to ask and answer, problems to solve, and issues to examine based on their own individual lives and needs, students find their own paths through the learning/teaching maze. When students are encouraged to become independent, self-motivated problem-solvers, the image of the learner and the image of the writer merge. At that point, with the freedom both to take risks with language and to employ language in personally meaningful ways, students discover for themselves the true power and potential of the writing process.

2 * In the world of the classroom

Letting the writing flow
Variety of teacher roles
Contexts for writing
Facing the school reality
Focusing on the 'basics'
Learning where to start
Language assessment survey

How do I get my students to write?
How do I get my students to write more?
What should I have them write about?

Teacher reference books are filled with ingenious answers to these questions. Teachers can offer their students lists of intriguing topic sentences, instruct them in a variety of 'shape' poem structures, ask them to speculate "what would happen if . . .", and employ a myriad other tried-and-true techniques to stimulate and generate their writing. Sometimes these approaches work and sometimes they don't. Sometimes they work with some students and not with others. The only constant is that using these techniques creates the need to use more. Rather than writing for their own reasons, stemming from the interests and needs of their own lives, students learn instead to depend on teachers for motivation. By the same token, teachers are caught in a 'Catch-22' situation because students have come to expect teacher direction. Without that direction, they don't write. With teacher direction, they write, but only to satisfy the criteria established by the teacher.

Letting the writing flow

With this in mind, when teachers ask how best to direct their students' writing, the inescapable answer is that they shouldn't. Writing is an active, independent process in which individuals attempt to understand and cope with their world and their lives. The more dependent student writers are on teachers, the less involved they are in a true writing process. By continuing to take responsibility for their student's motivation and by continuing to direct and mould

14

the scope and nature of what and how students write, well-meaning teachers actually perpetuate a strange hybrid of writing and conditioned response. Under these conditions, writing takes on the characteristics of an elaborate, filling-in-the-blanks, behaviorist exercise.

On the other hand, if students are going to assume responsibility for their own writing, the criteria for success in the classroom context need to be redefined. Students will more readily achieve their writing goals when they are involved in personal risk-taking. In other words, they need to internalize the understanding that they have the freedom to experiment with language, to use their own mode of language as a tool to unlock meaning, and to extend what they already know about language without unduly worrying about 'failing' or being wrong. Successful writers will often experiment, discover that the results don't fit their needs, and learn from that experience. In that sense, successful writers build 'failure' into their writing process.

Variety of teacher roles

For students to become successful risk-takers, teachers need to assume a variety of roles in the classroom writing dynamic.

As mentors, they demonstrate or model the process of meaningful writing. Rather than just a process through which stories, essays, and poems are churned out to be marked, writing is presented as a multi-faceted, open-ended activity in which adults and students take part for a variety of reasons and in a variety of ways across the curriculum. In that same role, they maintain a continuing dialogue with the younger writers, supporting, advising, and guiding — as directed by their students' needs.

As supervisors, they design an evaluation system that will reinforce rather than disenfranchise the prerogatives of their student writers. Implicit in such an evaluation system is the recognition that writing for learning is as valid a process as writing for communicating and that for both functions to flourish different criteria need to be maintained. In this role, teachers display respect for an individual's personal mode of expression, monitor how their students are functioning as writers, discover ways to diagnose their needs, and help them develop their own solutions to their own problems.

As editors, teachers establish and communicate an objective, knowledgeable, and experienced perspective. Their counsel helps student writers evaluate the effectiveness of their own writing and make the crucial decisions about assigning individual pieces to the different stages of further revision and publishing/marking or discontinuing the cycle and starting on another project. (Chapters 3 and 4 expand on the role of evaluation and offer a number of practical instruments for organizing, facilitating, and evaluating a writing process classroom program.)

Contexts for writing

In this kind of interdependent writing environment, material is generated in a variety of contexts. Some of these techniques can be maintained in almost any classroom program and for all students; some might be applicable for selected programs or introduced to only a few students. The following list details a few of the more popular formats.

Journals

Rather than have their students mechanically answer prescribed, predictable questions about content or mindlessly copy notes from the chalkboard, many teachers across the curriculum are turning to journal writing to facilitate and enhance the learning process. As well as requiring students to keep track of what they're doing, this type of approach encourages students on an individual basis to become actively involved in how and why they learn. Descriptions of a few of the more common forms of journals follow.

A writer's journal

Many writers carry a notebook in which they make random jottings whenever and wherever they feel the need. A sudden thought or idea, snippets of conversation, an inspired stream of consciousness, a vivid or moving experience, questions, interesting, colorful, or new words, effective images, and epigrams are just some of the content that such journals contain. Although the routine might not suit everyone, for students who find the practice productive and enlightening, a writer's journal can be carried and maintained at home or school and in any subject area. The journal serves as an obvious sourcebook for writing at all stages of the writing process.

A response journal

Growing numbers of teachers have integrated response journals into their language arts or English programs. A response journal is a notebook or folder in which students record their personal reactions to, questions about, and reflections on:

- what they read, view, listen to, and discuss;
- how they actually go about reading, viewing, listening, and discussing.

Just as a writing folder supports the writing process and is an essential tool in the formative and summative evaluation of both process and product, a response journal serves the reading process.

In an integrated program, however, the reading process combines elements of thinking, listening, speaking, writing, and viewing, as well as reading. The written response component of all of these elements can be combined and coordinated in the response journal. Students reflect on what they've been reading, doing, and talking about and then reflect on how and why they respond as they do. As they work through the response program, they are able to develop the awareness of and, eventually, the commitment to their own learning processes necessary to help them develop effective reading strategies.

A response journal is . . .

- a convenient, familiar, and flexible method for students to explore and reflect on their personal responses to such experiences as

  - independent reading
  - viewing a film or television program
  - listening to a readaloud
  - a small-group discussion

- a sourcebook of ideas, thoughts, opinions, and first drafts which can be 'mined' for later use in other contexts such as the writing folder

- a place to record observations and questions prior to a reading conference, and comments and suggestions derived from the conference

- a simple 'tracking' device for students to record what and how much they've read, and, after a small-group discussion, their individual perspectives on what was discussed or their roles in the discussion dynamics of the group

- a reference file to help both student and teacher monitor individual development and progress for both formative and summative evaluation purposes

- another way for individual students to 'dialogue' in written form with the teacher or their peers.

Since response journals serve so many different functions, an overview of their uses may appear complicated. Even tracing how they integrate the reading, writing, listening, speaking, and viewing aspects of English/language programs can seem confusing. In practice, on the other hand, response journals simplify, streamline, and organizie a comprehensive approach to personal response. (For a detailed explanation of how response journals operate, refer to *Response Journals*, Pembroke/Heinemann, 1990.)

The following samples provide a more concrete idea of what a response journal looks like when some of these learning objectives are translated into student outcomes. These abbreviated excerpts offer a glimpse into the variety of possible responses and the many functions served by response journals. Spelling errors have been corrected, but other stylistic features remain as they appeared in the original copy.

Sample responses

After completing an individual novel reading assignment, Jacqueline composed the following response. She had already chosen to discuss aspects of the novel on other occasions. Although she could have employed generic questions as a guide, she chose the topic and the content of this response on her own. As she analyzes certain characters and situations, she reveals her own personal connections with the story and the extent to which the story has made her reflect on her own life. In a natural, recursive manner, she weaves her way back and forth from story to real life. Implicit in this response is her confidence as an independent reader to unlock her own meaning in her own way.

Response to *No More Saturday Nights*

March 19

I couldn't believe Jim's father's attitude. He changed totally after the baby was born. Before that, he didn't even want to talk about the baby. After, he became a loving grandpa who loves taking care of Mason.

I don't see why Jim had sex with Vivian. He should've learned a lesson from having Mason. I'm not sure if he really likes her. He never mentioned he loves her. I wonder how Mason would feel about it. If I were in his shoes, I would not have been happy about my dad. I mean, just think about it, would anyone like to be a son or daughter of a mother whom his/her dad did not like? I personally don't think anyone would like it.

I wasn't expecting Cheryl [Mason's mom] to marry some 30 year old guy. I thought she wanted some sort of hunk!! She could actually get one easily, because she's beautiful. But maybe money is more important to her. Her family need money so badly that she almost sold the baby. I was really glad Jim finally got the baby back. It wasn't easy for him to get over it, but at least he tried.

I feel a kind of emptiness when one of my parents is not around. A kind of emptiness you can never fill in. I won't know what to do without my parents around anymore. I'm just a 13 year old, and I've never made any decisions (important ones) before, and that's one of the things I'm scared of when I'm all by myself. One of the things I wish to improve is my dependence. I sometime don't know what I want. I'm always unsure about what I'm going to do, or even if what I'm doing is right! My dad gets mad when he sees my unsureness.

Jackie J. (age 13)

Response journals can be used to integrate all aspects of the English program. In the next sample, a student decides to discuss the progress of a story she's writing. Her personal ownership of the creative process is evident when she writes about her excitement and satisfaction in producing the exact effects in a reader that she had intended. Equally fascinating is her reason for making this particular entry. She suggests that the act of writing puts her in touch with a concrete, author's perspective she might not otherwise possess.

Response to a writing period

April 17

I have become so ultimately fascinated by a mystery story that I have been writing that I decided to do a little response. As the story progresses I hope to build suspicion and I think I have succeeded. So far my story really hasn't told too much but I have an idea about a character who is a girl my age who returns to her birthplace where something of the supernatural happened. Today Mr. P read my story out loud to me, and to my surprise he interpreted it exactly how I wanted the story to be interpreted. So that really wowed me out. This story is really going to be a shocker, I mean something that you don't expect, something out of the unknown. I hope I succeed. I also want to create a memorable character with a memorable name. When I thought of that, a million names raced through my mind. I just thought that it would be interesting to respond to my story. This way I won't be so anxious for the ending, since I have the author's point of view.

Karen C. (age 13)

Individuals can comment in their response journals on the processes and dynamics of discussion groups and also use the forum to extend and deepen their understanding and appreciation of issues stimulated by discussions. In the following example, the initial small-group discussion on censorship began when the students learned that works by a well-known author of young-adult fiction were banned in some school districts. The author would be visiting their school the following week. As she describes the course of her reflections, this thirteen-year-old discovers that the issue is far more complex than she had originally thought. As she attempts to think her way through examples of vicarious experiences encountered in her viewing and reading, she tests, reformulates, and analyzes her own value system in a palpable and almost painful manner.

Response to a discussion

May 20

This was a great discussion! More thoughts and feelings came to my mind than during any other discussions. Mainly because there were different opinions, it pushed me to think a lot better than I usually do. At first I thought there should not be censorship in movies and books. You have a choice whether to see them or not. At this point, I think I've changed my mind a little. Now I'm sort of in the middle. In my point of view, books and movies we read and watch do affect our minds. It depends on the person. Say a person watched a movie or read a book which involves sexual abuse. That person might think it is exciting to have sex, or maybe he/she takes it as a guideline so he/she won't do it.

There was a part in Almost Japanese where Emma was forced to have sex with her boyfriend. As I was reading it, I found it horrible and I felt sorry for Emma. It's not like when they have sex scenes in movies where it shows all the excitement. In that part, it showed her helplessness and how she was hurt because her boyfriend did not like her personality, but her body. He did not show respect to her. When she told him she was not willing to do it, he still forced her to do it. I think that part is really important for the readers because it expressed how Emma felt toward Akira and her other boyfriend. She treasured Akira's love a lot more than making love to her other boyfriend. Akira's respectful manner is far more valuable than sex. You can have sex without love (rape). All Emma's boyfriend wanted from her was her body, and the experience. But Akira accepted the way she is. He loved her entirely, from top to bottom, her attitude, everything.

These are some of the points which have come strongly into my mind. After all I've said I don't think this book should be censored because it has a way of showing the value of love. After all these things I've said, I'm still not sure about censorship. Maybe I can never make up my mind. Who knows?

Arlene C. (age 14)

In a final example, the teacher read aloud the short story, "All Summer in a Day", by Ray Bradbury, and requested a personal response to the reading in the response journals. In the story, a young girl from Earth has been living in the perpetual rain of Venus. The sun comes out for one day every seven years. Just before the sun comes out, her spiteful classmates lock her in a closet.

The following entry was produced by a student who had been functioning in English for only eight months. Her first language was Cantonese. Since she knew that communicating meaning in the journals was pivotal and that surface errors were not corrected, the student had the confidence to reveal how closely she identified with the experience in the story and how deeply she felt about the natural world. In spite of her limited knowledge of English syntax and vocabulary, she is able to convey her feelings fluently and vividly.

Response to a readaloud ("All Summer in a Day")

If I was Margo, that girl came from Ohio since two years old and moved to a new planet Venus and seven years without sun, my feeling was very lonely, maybe homesick, although forget the shape or feel of sun, skies, the warmth of nature. When I was put in the closet I will try to think about the sun. If I had rain for seven years and suddenly the sun came out from those clouds, I must tried to enjoy, remember the happiness of the warm of the sun and thought about when I was two on Earth. Those memories and what reason why we need to move. Sun! Sun is a reddish-orange, oval-shaped, fireball that can give lives to animals and plants.

Alice C. (age 14)

Learning logs

As teachers have become more convinced about the importance of writing and reflecting in the learning/teaching process, they've started to use learning logs and work diaries more frequently in all grades and in all subject areas. In this approach, students keep day-to-day records of what they are doing in a particular subject area, how they feel about what they're doing, and what and how they're learning. Learning logs serve not only as another sourcebook for student writing but also as a reminder of the functional nature of writing. As with reading and writing journals, learning logs reinforce the role of writing as an essential element in the processing of experience. Since thinking and writing are intrinsically linked, students are encouraged to use their own form of language in a blend of expressive, transactional, and even poetic modes to examine, organize, 'think through', and reflect on what and how they learn. The process is ideosyncratic, recursive, unpredictable, and powerful.

Subject specific journals

Journal writing can link the entire curriculum and integrate the learning experience. Such subject areas as history, geography, or science can provide the questions, vicarious experiences, or illuminating connections that intrigue and inspire individual students. A theme from a content-area journal can easily be picked up in an English or language arts class to be processed and extended through further writing. In this way, the learning is internalized and deepened and the end result communicates to others another perspective on the original experience.

A first draft of the following story originated in the student's geography journal. A major earthquake in California inspired a spontaneous study of earthquakes. As part of the evaluation process, the student placed the vicarious experiences gleaned from the earthquake unit in the context of his own family and his immediate, earthquake-free neighborhood. For the purposes of the geography assignment, the narrative was acceptable in first-draft form. For his English class, however, the material was later revised. While in most respects the writing is reasonably typical of the age group, the origins of the story supply a series of specific, realistic, and dramatic details that create a striking and riveting effect not usually found even in real-life narratives.

Narrative developed from a geography journal entry

Earthquake

In the middle of doing my math homework up in my room, I happened to look at my clock. The moment it turned 6:31 p.m. the whole house started to rumble and the lights went out. Outside I heard the sound of car horns, the smashing of metal and glass, and a couple of blood-curdling screams.

"Everyone out of the house," my dad yelled, and I quickly found out why. The whole house was beginning to crumble right on top of us!

As we quickly dashed out of the house, our neighbors were also leaving their houses in panic. When we tried to shout to them to tell them not to go into the street, an ear-splitting house alarm went off and they couldn't hear us. As soon as they reached the street, it began to buckle and the entire street split in two lengthwise. We kneeled near the street on the grass; no one was hurt, yet.

In front of a couple of houses, the water lines burst through the ground. A lamp post fell near us. Luckily no one was in the way. Suddenly, we heard a shrill scream. Down the street, a man had a piece of balcony guard rail fall on him. He lay unconscious on his driveway. A couple of adults went to help him.

Then the whole neighborhood went silent. We didn't know what to do. Most of the houses were still standing, but they were in a dangerous condition. We didn't even think about going inside them. I saw only one person killed. A lamp post hit him. A lot of other people were hurt and my dog's leg was broken. We didn't know what to do. I just sat on the curb and my sister sat beside me and cried, while other adults went to look around. We were so scared. Could it happen again?

Kevin W. (age 11)

The subject for the next sample arose during a discussion of conservation. In groups of four or five, the students brainstormed lists of issues they felt needed to be addressed. They then focused on one of the issues and discussed problems and possible solutions.

One group entered into a heated debate on whaling. Following the discussion, the students were directed to respond in their journals not to the content but to the processes of the discussion. One student was so moved by the issue, however, that she carried the subject into her writing classroom and eventually produced the following narrative.

While the direct identification with the young animal is clearly expressed, the emotional content and balance of the piece is especially effective. This kind of narrative often slips into bathos. In this case, though, the discussion seems to have acted as an emotional release. Further reflection and crafting allowed the student to develop the restrained tone necessary to effectively present her sincere and deeply-felt point of view.

Narrative developed from a discussion on conservation

Whale Hunt

The pod of whales swims peacefully through the still waters, not hurting anyone or anything. The whales play like children in the sun-touched waters. A mother and her calf surface for a breath of fresh air. As they swim back down, they hear noises coming from the world above. The noises startle them and they swim as fast as they can towards the bottom. Hoping they are far enough down, they turn around to look back.

A large platform floats above them. Suddenly, a large net plunges into the water. The mother swerves to avoid it, but instead she snags herself in it. The calf moves closer but then backs off as the net and his mother slowly disappear into the world above. He lets out a shrill, squeaking sound, almost as if he were crying for her to come back. Then the net plunges into the water once again. He swerves and swims as fast as he can, just missing the net. When he turns around, the net has left. He looks up and the platform is moving now, heading towards land. The calf decides to follow it.

He follows for a long time before the platform reaches land. He surfaces to take a look. There he sees his mother lying helplessly at the mercy of four men with *large poles with very sharp, pointed ends. They begin to bring their arms up. Then, they send the poles crashing down deep into her body. She lets out a yelp and gives one last flick of her tail. Her eyes close and a stream of blood runs down her body. The calf swims alone to the bottom of the sea and fears the day they might come again.*

Cindy J. (age 14)

The following sample comes from a mathematics class where the teacher often employed a variety of hands-on activities designed to allow the students to learn through discovery. In their learning logs, the students kept track of what they did, reflected on the value or success of the activity, and tried to articulate how they felt about the experience.

During this particular class, the students drew three-dimensional views of a cylinder, constructed three-dimensional models from a two-dimensional pattern, and then tried to deduce the formula for finding the surface area of a cylinder. The teacher asked them to explain in their logs what they did, what they learned, and how they felt about the experience.

John's remarks indicate how valuable the concrete experience was to his eventual understanding and the extent to which he coped successfully, if informally, with a difficult concept. While his entry lacks specific formulae, it contains evidence of real comprehension.

Explanation of mathematics activity

April 28

What I Did

I drew a cylinder and tried to make it look like it was real. The ends didn't look right. Aaron's was really good. He even shaded it so it looked round. He's a pretty good artist. I tried the same thing on mine and it was okay. Then we cut cylinders out of paper and glued them together. The ends were hard to keep glued down. I thought mine looked like a rocket without the nose cone.

What I Learned

I saw the circles on the end all right, but I couldn't see the rectangle until the teacher said to take the models apart again. Then I could see that you did the circles on the end of the rectangle and then added them all together to get the area. I also learned how to shade round things.

How I Felt

I thought I did a good job on the cylinder. I understand how you have to find the area of a cylinder by finding the area of circles and rectangles first. I thought we were going to do something new, but we already knew how to do those things so it was easy.

John (age 12)

'Free' writing

Another technique for stimulating student writing, often called 'free' writing, is used primarily in language arts and English classes. Students who are 'blocked' and unable to write, stalled without inspiration or motivation, or genuinely tentative and unready to risk can find immediate release and relief by using this simple technique. A common approach to 'free' writing requires students to set a time limit, often ten to twenty minutes, place pencil or pen to paper, and commence non-stop, written, free association. The key rules are that once started the student continues to write until the time limit is over, that conventional concerns such as punctuation, spelling, and handwriting are disregarded, and that the teacher need never read the result. As the name suggests, this technique 'frees' students by allowing their thoughts and feelings to spill out spontaneously on to the page, unfettered by worries about form, structure, content, or censure.

Since the technique can easily be misused and overused, caution is necessary. For a time, teachers were encouraged to use sustained, stream-of-consciousness writing regularly, even daily, with all students in the class in the belief that increased 'time on task' alone would improve fluency. Although student enthusiasm for this kind of enforced diary-keeping quickly dried up and negative attitudes toward writing counter-balanced any initial benefits, the practice continued.

The following fragment is taken from a student's first experience with 'free' writing. The technique was suggested to her because she was having difficulty getting personally involved in her writing. Although she had drafts at various stages of revision, the topics didn't excite her and she had no new ideas. As she begins her writing, a preoccupation with relationships surfaces. (Mistakes in spelling and punctuation have been retained.)

Response to 'free' writing experience

> I hope this works. My teacher told me to do this when I told him I had writer's block. I have no idea at all. I thought about writing about Korea and Canada. The differences between the two. I'm running out of ideas. I'm suppost to keep on writing but I don't think I'm going to be able to. I don't know if I like Kirk anymore. It's hard to tell. I don't think I'm going to be able to like him intill the summer. That's when he said he would go out with me . . .
>
> Greene Y. (age 13)

In the next fragment, the same student expresses concern about the form of the exercise itself and the lack of conventional form in her writing. As fatigue begins to play havoc with the surface features of the writing, she spontaneously turns to another relationship.

> ... Only five minits has gone by. I've had so many spelling mistake and my writing is so messy. I don't know if this is going to work or not I don't think so. Barb has just ruin it She stopped me to give her a pen I don't think it should matter though. I really don't like the person she likes. He buggs me so much. I think I'm going to not be with her so much if when she goes out with him. Personally I think he's a jerk ...

By the end of the 'free' writing, she has stopped worrying about surface features and returns again to express her sincere frustration with the personal situation mentioned earlier.

> ... I don't know if I should put this in my rough part of my folder or not or throw it away. If Barb reads it she'd get mad because about what I said about Garry. She think he so nice. She's so wronge.

After discussing the results of the experiment with her teacher, the student developed a first-draft essay on friendship that eventually evolved into the following poem. Although the theme and the sentiments are familiar, the freshness of the images and the genuineness of the feeling invest the poem with a unique flavor and life of its own. Through the 'free' writing, the student discovered a theme she needed to explore and unearthed memories and emotions she wanted to express.

Poem developed from 'free' writing experience

Best Friends

How can I repay you?
You have always been there for me.
When I get sad, you get tears in your eyes.
When I'm happy, you jump up and down more than I
   do.
You always know when I need help.
Then, you're always at my side.
I never have to ask you for advice.
You'll just give it to me and you'll always be right.
You're the only one who can make me laugh and feel
   better
When I'm sad,
You always say the right thing at the right time.
When I want to talk, you will just listen.
If I have nothing to say, you will keep the conversation
   alive.
I've always loved going out together with you.
It has never been dull.
You make me laugh so much that I cry.
Nobody else can make me laugh so much.
I love when we're sharing secrets.
I feel closer to you during those times.
Even when we're in a fight, you keep my secrets.
They seem to get buried inside you as soon as you hear
   them.
When I'm with my other friends, I still feel alone.
I have to put on a show for them.
When I'm with you I know that you're with me.
I can always act myself.

> *My friendship with you means the world to me.*
> *I don't know what I would do without you.*
> *Our friendship will last forever.*
> *You will always be my best friend.*
>
> *Greene Y. (age 13)*

First-hand experience

In keeping with their emergent reading and writing development in the early primary grades, students talk about and dictate stories revolving around the theme they know best — their own lives. With little urging needed and using their own mode of language, students eagerly recount their experiences with family, friends, pets, holidays, trips, and a host of other personal topics and issues. This kind of writing is commonly called 'language experience.'

At the same time, the fiction being read to them and the fiction they begin to read themselves have a profound impact on their understanding and use of language. This influence becomes apparent as the syntax, vocabulary, and themes from literature are mirrored in their own writing. A healthy balance of personal narratives and stories patterned after literature is maintained. From late primary and through the junior grades, however, they're encouraged to become even more creative, possibly in response to and in imitation of the amount of children's fiction being read. Wildly inventive fictional narratives usually result. In the transitional years and in preparation for the perceived demands of the secondary curriculum, intermediate students are steered away from narrative writing and into the expository mode.

Personal relationships

Regardless of the grade level or the form of expression, students should continue to explore and reflect on their personal lives. The most revered cliché about writing directs neophytes to write about what they know best. At all ages and at all stages of development, students need frequent opportunities to explore the themes to which they can most readily relate. Writing is recursive and so is interest in those early themes. If students are allowed to tap their own personal experience, the language will flow. Besides, their fascination with and attempts to understand such influences as family and friends continue all their lives. The perspective that age, reflection, and introspection offer continually adds new pieces and added dimensions to their personal 'jigsaw puzzles.' Professional writers return again and again to their early years and those pivotal relationships and formative experiences that contributed to the development of their personal value systems and their particular world view. With encouragement, students of all ages will continue to respond to this endlessly intriguing, every-changing source of wonder.

When a student writes from experience, the intense nature of personal reflection holds the potential to propel the individual from discovery to discovery. Meaning is the focal point, intrinsically, and the form of the writing is forged from that experience. In the two samples that follow, a family relationship is examined. In the first, the student probes the trauma of death. The power of the writing derives from the sincerity of the feeling, the cumulative, cathartic effect of the vivid, apt, and graphic details, and the slow, deliberate unfolding of final comprehension. The writing is understated, matter-of-fact, and irresistible.

Reflecting on family relationships

Grandpa

My grandpa, Charlie Luoma, was my only grandpa. He built our cottage one year and then, a week after, he had a stroke. We brought him up to visit a few times. He was in the hospital and then a nursing home. I used to go and visit him all the time. I would take him to the cafeteria and he would get a coffee and I would get some pie. But then he died, on Mother's Day (a real treat for my mom). That day, we had relatives over for dinner and we went to visit grandpa after dinner. When we arrived there, my mom and my Uncle Desmond and

Uncle Ray were informed that he had died a half hour before. My dad took all the kids home and we waited for my mom and uncles to get home.

A few days later, I missed school so that I could go to the funeral. I had never been to a funeral before and I wasn't really sure if I really wanted to go. I went. It was an open casket at Ogden Funeral Homes. I have never felt the way I felt when I looked down at him. He was pure white from the powder that was on him, and he was cold. I held his hands and I flicked his ear lobes like I did when I was a little girl. He was wearing a suit and a tie that I had given my father for Father's Day. He was to be cremated so I wrote a letter to him and requested for it to be cremated with him. At the ceremony I cried and my older sister and my brother laughed at me. My grandpa's ashes are to be spread under the cottage this year. Every time I drive by Ogden Funeral Homes I smell the powder that was all over my grandpa's face and hands.

I love you, grandpa!

Dana D. (age 13)

In a final example, an accomplished young poet of the same age and from the same classroom also examines a family relationship. While the language is rich in exquisite metaphor, the same innocent fascination and sincere affection so evident in "Grandpa" also provide the source of this poem's power and vitality. The form of expression is different, but the process of reflection and the development of understanding are similar. Although these students had often approached the theme of family in their school careers, they still had much to learn and say.

Exploring a family relationship through metaphor

Epigram on Abu (Father)

I think
my Abu
is like a lion
who does not
live in the jungle
but with me.

I think
my Abu is
mysterious because
he has a village
of poetry
hidden under
his skin.

The way he feels
would not fall on paper
but
would melt
inside him.

Sometimes I want to know
why my Abu
does the things he does
but I'm afraid
when I find out
something might explode.

Mariam D. (age 13)

Computer technology keeps producing more and more tools with intriguing possibilities for the writing classroom. Communication by computer modem, for example, has almost limitless potential. In the following example, students at two different levels and from two different schools became engaged in a free-flowing process that included aspects of letter-writing, personal response, mentoring, and 'buddy authoring'. As students took over responsibility for the interactions, the results were often unexpected and impressive.

The project started when students from a Grade 8 class at one school were paired with students from a Grade 3 class at another school. An electronic bulletin board system made it possible for the students to interact without ever meeting. They composed on computers and then uploaded the results to the electronic bulletin board. Whenever it was convenient, the other school downloaded the material and responded at a later date. After an initial period in which the individuals from the two classes exchanged greetings and some personal information, the older students began supplying reader response to stories written by the younger students. When directed by their partners, the older students also offered revising and editing assistance.

After reading a story called "A Girl Who Loved Everyone", sent by her young partner, the older student sent back the following response. The story dealt with a little girl who had a difficult day with her teachers and friends until everyone made up and ended the day with a party. In the response, the focus on content and the informal, conversational tone were typical of the modem interactions.

Grade 8 response to Grade 3 story

Hi, Kavita! I'm glad you sent me your story. While I was reading it, I thought about my own teachers and friends. When the two friends got in a fight, it reminded me of when I got in a fight with one of my friends. We made up the next day.

Although I enjoyed your story, I was left with some

questions. I wondered why the girl was late for school and why she got into a fight with her friend. You never explained those details. I also wondered why the little girl was having so much trouble with her teachers and friends if she loved everybody. It didn't seem fair.

Well, you certainly got me thinking with your story. That's all for now. Bye! (Donna)

With one pair of students, a simple request initiated an extended and complex interchange. The younger student asked her older partner to write her a story. The older student (Karen C., age 14) spontaneously sent back this lovely example of creative storytelling.

Older student's story

Once upon a time there was a pink fairy. Her name was Cheryl. One day Cheryl broke her wing and fell into a tree. As she was crying, a butterfly came by and invited Cheryl to stay with her until her wing became better. When the time came and Cheryl's wing was all better, she became such good friends with the butterfly that she stayed and lived with her. And they lived happily ever after. (Karen)

This storytelling episode stimulated Karen's own creativity. Shortly afterwards, she produced a rough draft of a poem designed for a younger audience. After revising and editing the poem to her own satisfaction, she asked permission to send it to the Grade 3 class for a response. Notice how clearly she has identified with the mind and world of a young child, to the extent that the imagery emerges naturally and spontaneously. Simple rhyming couplets and strong rhythm add to the emotional appeal.

Older student's poem

Cecelia's Rainbow

It's cold and rainy, there's nothing to do.
Mommy is busy, my friend has the flu.
There's nothing to do on this miserable day.
It's not even sunny to go out and play.
So, here I sit all bored and alone.
I'm still too young to talk on the phone!
Maybe I'll go and talk to the cat.
Nope, that won't work, it's having a nap.
I sit on the couch and twiddle my hair.
I look to the window, what's that out there?
The rain has stopped, the sun's in the sky.
As I look up, up, up, there are colors! Oh, my!
And how lovely they are, so nice and pretty.
I never thought I'd see this living in the city!
"Mommy, Mommy, what's that I see?"
"It's a rainbow, Cecelia. What else could it be?"
"Can I touch it? Smell it? Taste it? Is it real?"
"Cecelia, don't be silly! Scoot now, I'm cooking a
    meal."
I run back to the window and look in the air.
My eyes fill with tears, the rainbow's not there!
I hope it comes back, I hope very soon,
A rainbow with colors of every balloon!
As I mope and I sulk, there's nothing to do.
Mommy is busy, my friend has the flu.

Karen

38

The teacher of the primary class read the poem aloud to his class and asked for their responses. These were sent directly back to Karen. The following two samples were typical and display how the younger students had internalized the idea of personal response through the interaction with their partners.

The chapter on evaluating student-written poetry has sample evaluations based on "Cecelia's Rainbow" (pages 84-86).

Grade 3 response: sample one

That poem had a pattern. Cecelia was sad, then happy, then sad again. I thought the poem was nicely done. If Cecelia was real I would feel sorry for her. How old was Cecelia anyway? The only reason I'm asking is because she wasn't allowed to talk on the phone. I think she must have been young, maybe two or three years old.

Grade 3 response: sample two

I really liked the poem. I felt sad too when my mom left me with my grandma at night. I liked the part when Cecelia says, "Can I touch it? Smell it? Taste it? Is it real?" Who told you to write the poem and how did you think it up?

At this point, Karen had an opportunity few authors receive. After writing for a specific audience and receiving their immediate reactions to her work, she was able to bring the process full circle by expressing her own feelings and answering the questions her audience had posed. Karen's sense of authority over her own work and her assurance of her own role as author are evident in the following remarks she sent back.

Response to response

To: Mr. S's Class

From: Karen C. (author of "Cecelia's Rainbow")

First of all, I would like to thank everyone for your comments. I really appreciate the time and effort you took to write them. I'd also like to answer a few questions so you can understand the poem more.

A few of you asked why I named the little girl Cecelia. Well, to be honest, I really don't know. It just seemed to pop into my head when I was writing. Another person asked what was the name of the friend who had the flu. Well, the friend who had the flu really didn't have a name. It was just supposed to be a small character in the story. However, you can give that friend any name you want.

Lili, you asked who told me to write the poem. No one told me to write this poem. I just sat down one day and wrote "Cecelia's Rainbow".

Tyler, you asked if Cecelia had a brother or sister. I never really thought about it, but because she's bored and lonely, I would say she doesn't. But she does have a cat! Too bad it was sleeping.

I would like to say one more thing. Harmeet, you made a pretty good guess about Cecelia's age. When I made up Cecelia, I wanted her to be about four or five years old, someone who is very curious and doesn't know much.

Once again I would like to thank you all for your comments and questions.

This example of the use of electronic communication demonstrates an essential principle. Technology can only assist a process, not create it. The success of modem interchange hinges on the same key as the writing process itself; namely, how receptive and adaptable the process is to developing student ownership and to meeting individual needs.

Facing the school reality

Although teachers have developed a number of approaches to the development of a writing process, all too easily these approaches become ends in themselves. In spite of their commitment to a process orientation, teachers find that the nature and operation of schools tend to short-circuit process and substitute a powerful imperative for and an unwavering focus on product. Schools, at best, offer a difficult, almost hostile, environment for writers. Restrictions, distractions, and a variety of contradictory pressures not only complicate but actually militate against the writing process. Teachers are constantly picking their way through a minefield of school-based pressures, such as the following:

- inflexible reporting procedures, shortened reporting periods, demand for marks, inappropriate report cards

- fragmented language programs (spelling/grammar periods), limited time for writing, limited access to computers, rotary timetables, burgeoning curriculum/shrinking timetable

- administrative and/or parental expectations ('back to the basics'), emphasis on surface features of product, 'accountability' (school-wide marking, publishing routines)

- lack of continuity and consistency (writing program undermined by approaches to writing in other subject areas and by previous programs)

- inappropriate environment (frequent interruptions, lack of reading/writing materials, crowded classrooms, restricted space).

For these reasons, using the writing behavior of professional writers as a model for classroom writing can certainly instruct but never direct classroom practice. Professional writers are personally involved, self-motivated, egocentric, and autonomous. They make their own choices and their own compromises. The crucial and, often, misunderstood or ignored difference between their world and that of student writers or English teachers is context. Professional writers write in the real world. Students write (and teachers teach) in the tangled, frustrating, and sometimes baffling world of schools.

Focusing on the 'basics'

At this point, two essential questions need to be answered. What are the guiding principles of the writing process and how much of that process can be implemented in the unique context of a school?

In the first place, the writing process isn't a 'thing'. Whenever a certain set of procedures, a designated series of steps, or a specific technique becomes synonymous with a definition of writing, the process itself inevitably becomes subverted. Teachers who slavishly follow a specific model of writing are doomed to disappointment and disillusionment. *The writing process in schools is actually a state of mind supported by beliefs about learning in general and the nature of writing specifically.* Questions such as whether or not students should produce picture books, draft in a specific way, compose in groups, or peer-edit are all subordinated to these beliefs. In and of themselves, these beliefs are neither complicated nor difficult to translate into practice, despite the considerable difficulty that arises when that practice is placed in the context of school language programs.

The first rule of writing is that there are no rules. Since people write to make sense of and to cope with their world (and ultimately themselves), any procedural rules a teacher sets up to facilitate the writing process are automatically subject to change without notice. If, by definition, writing must always be functional, the process must remain functional as well. Demands about the length or genre of a particular piece of writing, how much time is spent on it, or how many drafts it has to go through must necessarily conform to the needs of the individual writer and the purposes for writing. Merely to state that writing is recursive and individualistic doesn't begin to sketch how haphazard, egocentric, and just plain messy the process looks to an outsider — or how difficult it is to fit it into the regulated, public, and carefully groomed world of the school.

Maintaining priorities

The enormous complexities involved in bringing such a shifting, subjective process to life in a busy classroom filled with thirty or more entirely different individuals can be daunting.

- What procedures should be set in place?
- When should these procedures be short-circuited?
- Won't students take advantage of rules that aren't really binding?
- What is purposeful writing to a student writer?

Questions such as these would give pause to any teacher. When one adds to that perspective an understanding that the entire structure of any writing classroom rests on its all-pervasive evaluation system, the nature of the daily compromises teachers have to make becomes apparent.

That complexity is the main reason teachers need to write themselves. No single model of writing instruction is sufficiently comprehensive to address the myriad problems teachers encounter or direct the many decisions they need to make. Sometimes, a particular option is exercised simply because, as a writer, it makes sense. That balance between a teacher's set agenda and a writer's intuition can be achieved only if the teacher writes. Teachers are encouraged to 'model' for their students the writing behaviors that grow out of their own personal writing experiences. As valuable as these demonstration lessons may be, the essential benefit a teacher derives from writing is the confidence to apply the 'no-rules' strategy when necessary to preserve the basic integrity of the classroom writing program.

Principles of a writing process program

The predominant characteristics associated with the writing process may need clarification. The following principles represent an ideal state. In most classroom writing environments, some students will have already internalized these principles and will be using them to support their own growth as writers. Most students, however, will have little understanding of what these principles actually represent or how they might be applied to their own writing.

Although the following principles offer a great deal of flexibility in what, where, when, and how students write, given the nature and underlying purpose of schools, *not* writing is never an option. That qualification is the first compromise the writing process undergoes in a school setting.

A writing process is in place when students feel encouraged to . . .

- determine the purpose and audience for their writing

- explore ideas and 'think through' concepts by writing for themselves

- self-select the content and the form of their own writing

- develop a sense of belonging to a community of writers and appreciate the value of collaboration, at times, for generating and testing ideas and revising and editing material

- evalute the effectiveness of their own writing, including making decisions about sharing, publishing, and submitting specific pieces for marking.

With so much emphasis on the value of ownership and a writer's sense of autonomy, these principles find an uneasy home in an environment in which group standards are usually the norm. Complicating the picture even further is the fact that students have had a variety of different writing experiences and often differing views of what writing is all about. Teachers need to assess these experiences to get a better idea of where to start and how to proceed with their student writers.

Learning where to start

The pulse of the classroom is subject to numerous restrictions and pressures that quicken and shorten the natural, spontaneous, and admittedly messy nature of the writing process. Obviously, the more a process is truncated, the less effective that process becomes. In fact, rather than encouraging growth in writing, a truncated process often turns into a source of frustration that interferes with both short-term and long-term writing goals. Depending on age and experience, many students already possess a clear idea of what writing is, a specific attitude toward writing in school, and a set of proven strategies to cope with the demands made on them.

If students have had little experience with a true writing process, changing their learned beliefs and firmly-established behaviors will take understanding, patience, and time. Even if they have been exposed to some kind of process orientation, too many deadlines for too many 'polished' pieces of writing may have already driven them to think in terms of expediency. After all, the first lesson students learn in school is to give adults what they ask for.

Given the complex nature of the classroom writing environment, quickly getting to know what kinds of language programs students have come through and how they view themselves in terms of processing language becomes crucial. Instead of dispensing a series of so-called basic skills tests and then haphazardly forming group and individual profiles from the results, teachers can gain better and more useful data by going straight to the primary source, their students.

Who knows better than the students themselves the kinds of language or writing experiences they've had, how confident they feel about the demands made on them, and the strengths and problems they've discovered as they've worked through language programs? At the same time, students will receive the crucial message that their perceptions are trusted and their opinions important. A simple survey can become a first step in 'empowering' students.

Language assessment survey

The sample survey on pages 46-47, *My Memorable Moments in English*, is divided into two sections. When the results from Part One are collated, they should supply a group profile of language-related activities, all of them characteristic of an integrated and process-oriented program. This kind of data will help the teacher to decide how various activities should be introduced and paced with a specific group of students.

Part Two is more personal and the results remain confidential. What emerges from the answers is a detailed profile of how frequently and freely each student processes language, how each feels about past language-related experiences, and the reading and viewing episodes each has enjoyed. With positive self-image as the essential goal of effective learning behavior, this initial information can help a teacher decide how best to build or reinforce positive attitudes toward writing with each individual student.

My Memorable Moments in English (Part One)
(over the past few years)

Name: _____ Class: _____ Date: _____

	Never	A Few Times	Often	Very Often
1. An author visited my classroom	1	2	3	4
2. I chose my own reading material	1	2	3	4
3. I took part in reading conferences with my teacher	1	2	3	4
4. I took part in reading conferences with my peers	1	2	3	4
5. My teacher read to the class	1	2	3	4
6. A storyteller visited the classroom	1	2	3	4
7. I took part in small-group discussions	1	2	3	4
8. I chose what I wanted to write about	1	2	3	4
9. I took part in writing conferences with my teacher	1	2	3	4
10. I took part in writing conferences with my peers	1	2	3	4
11. I kept a writing folder	1	2	3	4
12. I used a computer for writing	1	2	3	4
13. I took part in "buddy reading"	1	2	3	4
14. I took part in "buddy authoring"	1	2	3	4
15. The classroom/school published my writing	1	2	3	4

My Memorable Moments in English (Part Two)
(over the past few years)

Name: _____ Class: _____ Date: _____

	Not at All			Very
1. How much I enjoy reading for pleasure outside school	1	2	3	4
2. How much I enjoy reading in school	1	2	3	4
3. How much I think of myself as an author	1	2	3	4
4. How much I enjoy reading for pleasure outside school	1	2	3	4
5. How much I enjoy writing in school	1	2	3	4
6. How confident I am about my reading	1	2	3	4
7. How confident I am about my writing	1	2	3	4
8. How comfortable I am writing with a computer	1	2	3	4
9. How comfortable I am talking in small groups	1	2	3	4
10. How comfortable I am talking to adults	1	2	3	4

Some novels I have enjoyed are: _____

_____

Some magazines I enjoy reading are: _____

_____

Some television programs I like to watch are: _____

_____

3 * The writing process toolkit

The various strategies, techniques, and instruments in this chapter have a specific function. The frenetic, harried, and product-driven nature of school environments and the delicate, introspective, and time-consuming nature of the writing process make it difficult for teachers to stitch the two together. The 'tools' in the following sections are designed to build bridges between the world of professional writers and the world of writers in schools. Implicit in this task is the understanding that, although related, the two worlds are inherently different. At the core of this difference lies the complex issue of evaluation.

'Writing' some wrongs

People write to make sense of and to cope with their world. As is the case with so much of human growth, growth in writing is synonymous with risk-taking. Ironically, in schools, the more tentative, personal, and subjective the writing, the more it gets marked. Moreover, as much as teachers talk about the value of process, when it comes time to mark, they focus on the product. In other words, the more students tend to take risks in their writing in order to make sense of their world, the more teachers tend to discourage those risks through the overt value system of marks. Narratives, personal essays, opinion pieces, and poetry all fall under this shadow. On the other hand, the kind of functional writing students engage in to cope with their world is hardly ever valued (i.e., marked). Brainstorming ideas, making lists and notes, planning, generating questions, and informally exploring ideas through writing come under this category.

In fact, writing programs are often riddled with so many inconsistencies and mixed messages that a teacher's best efforts to pursue a process orientation are effectively neutralized. In the context of school priorities and pressures, the following situations may be understandable, but they still undermine and thwart a process curriculum for writing:

- teachers appreciate that writing is a personal and individual process and yet continue to insist on specific topics and themes from all students, as well as a specific number of drafts;
- they understand the recursive nature of writing but still organize writing programs and schedules on a linear basis;
- they talk about the value of ideas but stress surface features such as spelling and neat handwriting during marking;
- they ask students to collaborate but assign marks on an individual and competitive basis;
- they acknowledge the benefits of diagnostic and formative evaluation but spend most of their time gathering grades for summative purposes;
- they have students keep writing folders to supply evidence of a process over time but assign grades only to individual pieces of writing;
- they encourage self- and peer-evaluation but, in fact, demonstrate that in the final analysis only teacher evaluation 'counts'.

For these and other reasons, students and teachers alike are uncomfortable with the writing process. Teachers are forced into a "do as I say, not as I do" rationale, and students can't make sense out of any of it. All they know is what they've learned — go for the marks!

Some educators dismiss marks and any kind of evaluation other than self-evaluation as nonsense and counter-productive to the learning process. For people not working directly in a classroom or who are not responsible for administering a school, that kind of stance probably makes a lot of sense. Teachers, however, don't need more fanciful flights from reality. Better than anyone else, teachers understand the limitations of their learning/teaching environments. What they do need is a way to reverse the negative features of evaluation.

That's why the evaluation system has to be tailor-made for a process-oriented program. By recognizing the power of evaluation to direct learning and allowing the evaluation system to support the criteria for a process classroom, teachers can, at the very least, minimize the inconsistencies and mixed messages. In the sections that follow, evaluation criteria are embedded in each process and are intrinsic to the development of a process orientation.

Setting up the writing folder

Whether a student uses a file folder, a loose-leaf binder, or a notebook, the function of that folder should be to mirror and facilitate the writing process. (See pages 97-99 for additional information on how and why these folders are used.) For a number of reasons, a practical, usable writing folder is absolutely essential if the writing process is to flourish in classrooms. Students and teachers alike need that 'mirror' to help them reflect on and learn from specific, individual writing patterns over time. Students need the organizational and record-keeping assistance a folder offers and the freedom to pursue a recursive, ever-changing investigation into meaning that a folder should also offer. Teachers want a folder to stimulate the kinds of activities they perceive as beneficial to young writers and they also need the objective evidence a folder contains to make summative decisions.

Tracking writing activities — student sample

The following five-day record from a student's response journal describes her writing activities during a series of English classes. Her tracking entries illustrate the kinds of behaviors a teacher would like to encourage over time and eventually reward through the use of marks.

Day One

Charlene asked me to read her piece on boyfriends. I read it and we talked a bit about how I don't think it's fair for her to dump on someone everybody will recognize and then we talked a lot about boyfriends other people have. I also told her I didn't know why she was writing something like that. She went off to work on it and I pulled my story on drugs out of my folder and started to rewrite the ending. But I started to think about a TV show I saw last night about a guy who had an argument with his stepfather and ran away from home. Charlene saw it, too. She knew a guy who got into some trouble and had to hide out. Just like Ponyboy in The Outsiders. It's an old book but I like it. I asked the teacher if I could go look for it in the library. By the time I got back the class was just about over.

Day Two

I read some of The Outsiders. I had forgotten that Ponyboy was an orphan. I started to make a list of how my life would be different if I were an orphan. It's really interesting. I have a conference with the teacher tomorrow. I asked Sean if he'd help me with the ending of the story on drugs. He read it out loud and I suddenly realized I'd need an opening before I write the ending. It's boring. I don't know why I started it. I asked him if he'd ever known any orphans. He talked a bit about how his mom died. I start to wonder what it would be like if my parents died. Really morbid. I started to write a story about it, but it was boring.

Day Three

I asked the teacher if it's fair to write about real people and real things that happened. He asked me like what and I said like about my grandmother dying. He said sure. I wrote the whole period.

Day Four

I wrote the whole period.

Day Five

Charlene read my story and she cried. I think it's the best thing I ever wrote. It really shows the way I felt. I don't think I want to change anything in it.

Paula (age 12)

In this series of journal entries, Paula describes how she has been exploring various aspects of the writing process. She has taken part in peer-conferences to discuss the work of others and has initiated conferences to discuss her own writing. She has also been reworking and shaping material. While definitely highly personal, recursive, and difficult for an outsider to follow, the process has produced a valuable experience and a piece of writing that genuinely touches others. Paula will probably return the story on drugs to the exploratory section of her writing folder and take her story about her grandmother through to the publishing/marking stage.

To preserve the process that produced such an effective product, teachers should consider organizing the summative evaluation (marking) of writing with due regard to both process and content.

Marking the writing folder

From time to time, students will hand in pieces of writing for marking. (The sections on marking narrative and expository writing, pages 68-74, and student-written poetry, pages 76-84, offer some practical ideas and instruments.) The marks derived from these pieces, however, should never constitute the entire grade for writing. If process is to flourish, the components in that process need to be articulated, periodically reviewed, and also marked. The final grade for writing would be some combination of a process mark and a product mark. In the example the follows, the balance between process and product is half and half. If a teacher wanted to emphasize process over product, that balance could be adjusted accordingly. Although the product marks are accumulated as students hand in material for marking, the entire writing folder is reviewed and marked only at prescribed intervals and only when enough time has elapsed for a process to unfold and growth to occur. Many teachers find that a four- to six-week period is sufficient.

In the sample marks summary, four components of process are emphasized. Even the generation of rough or exploratory writing should be valued. Exploratory writing could take a variety of forms, including brainstorming lists, stream-of-consciousness writing ('free' writing), or rough fragments.

In the revising stage, marks are given for engaging in peer- or adult-conferences to discuss both a student's own work and that of other students. Techniques for keeping track of these collaborations are provided on page 63. In this model, since revising is accepted as a sophisticated and complex experience and far more difficult for students to apprehend and practise than editing, that component is appropriately weighted.

In the editing stage, since collaboration is also an objective, marks are awarded for holding editing conferences as well as for submitting a 'clean' manuscript for publishing and/or marking. Again, to encourage as much material as possible proceeding to a final stage, the teacher should reward the student for simply submitting a sufficient number and variety of pieces for marking. Although the various features of this kind of marking scheme may seem relatively complicated at first, the actual instrument is reasonably straightforward and simple to use.

This kind of evaluation system has a double purpose. It both stimulates a process orientation and assesses it. To achieve that double purpose, students need to know and understand the criteria by which their efforts will be judged. For this reason, a copy of the evaluation criteria should remain in every student's writing folder. To be effective, as well, such a system has to be easily maintained and administered. The payoff for teachers is that much of the tracking and pre-marking organizing is done by the students. Another simple instrument for keeping track of the writing in the folder as well as the stage of the writing is provided on page 57.

Sample Writing Folder Marks Summary

Name: _____ Class: _____

Evaluation Period: from _____ to _____

A. Process

Exploratory Stage (rough drafts)	more than		sufficient		less than	
a. Sufficient number	5	4	3	2	1	0
b. Sufficient variety (genres)	5	4	3	2	1	0
Revising Stage (drafting process)	frequently		usually		seldom	
a. Incorporates peer/adult response to own material	5	4	3	2	1	0
b. Offers assistance to others	5	4	3	2	1	0
c. Shapes and reworks material	10	8	6	4	2	0
Editing Stage (proofreading process)	frequently		usually		seldom	
a. Applies peer-editing strategies	5	4	3	2	1	0
b. Presents a final, print-ready draft	5	4	3	2	1	0
Marking/Publishing Stage	more than		sufficient		less than	
a. Sufficient number	5	4	3	2	1	0
b. Sufficient variety	5	4	3	2	1	0

B. Product

Title	Type	Date	Mark

Total = [   ] /50 + [   ] /50 = [   ] /100   Average = _____
                                                                    50

Writing Folder Contents

Name: _____   Class: _____

Title	Type	*Stage: E ☐ D ☐_____ P ☐	**Mark	Date Marked

* E = Exploratory
D = Draft (a check mark for each draft)
P = Polished (ready for marking)
** Only for polished pieces handed in for marking

The student keeps track of and enters all the information. Since the teacher will use this sheet to assign writing folder marks for number and variety of exploratory and polished material, it's in the student's self-interest to maintain the record. The record also proves useful during student-teacher conferences for reflecting on the pattern of writing in the folder. Since individual sheets easily become lost or crumpled in some types of writing folders, many teachers staple or glue record sheets like this on to stiff cardboard for durability and for easy reference. The forms may even be printed on card stock. As with so many of these strategies for maintaining a writing process, the form of the instrument needs to clearly match the function.

Collaborating on revising and editing

A community of writers is built on trust. In effect, for a writing process to flourish in a classroom context, that classroom must become decentralized. Many of the motivational, advisory, decision-making, and evaluative roles formerly held by the teacher need, as much as possible, to be assumed by the students themselves. The form of the collaborative process rests on the function. Collaboration among students develops naturally as they take control of their own writing, have something to say, and require assistance to say it. In this regard, writing is a true problem-solving activity.

In the following case study, a twelve-year-old writer describes a specific writing experience in which she tries to translate and communicate her feelings as stimulated by a picture. Although an experienced and confident poet (with some of her poetry published in a small magazine with a Southeast Asia readership), she had never gone through a revision process before. She ordinarily transcribed her stream-of-consciousness reflections. At two key points in this process, the writer discusses her draft with a peer.

The picture in question was one of a series on her classroom wall highlighting environmental issues. The nighttime photograph showed a dark, slender tree outlined in the foreground. Behind the tree, and beneath a full, glowing moon, an oil refinery with gleaming glass and metal turrets shone a ghostly, translucent, pastel-pink and yellow under the harsh lights of the compound and the moon's eerie illumination.

The student explains:

I was looking around trying to think of something to write about. My eyes spotted a picture hanging on the wall. I had seen that picture many times before, but I had never noticed the different views it had.

Her first draft was a personal response constructed partly as a poem and partly as a prose reaction.

First draft

Black tree
The dust
and the moon behind
Shining like gold,
drowning in the color
of the huge sky.

As your mind is falling into the feeling of being there to look at it and to capture the movement you notice the lights behind. It kind of spoils the feeling right there.

Triangular shapes
the tall buildings and the thin towers
different colors turning bright
creating a forest

But then again

It doesn't spoil the feeling, it creates a new one.

Mariam D. (age 13)

At this point, Mariam wasn't sure what to do with her response. She wasn't satisfied with it, and yet she wasn't sure what approach to take. Mariam enlisted a peer to read the response and give her a reaction. The peer suggested that the poem might fall into two parts or two views and suggested that the structure and development of the poem follow that direction. Mariam responded. Part description, part spontaneous commentary on the picture and the feelings it evokes, the second draft ends with a series of questions.

Second draft

Two Views in One Picture

Part One:

Black tree
the dust and the moon overlapping
shining like gold
drowning in the color of the huge sky

My mind is falling into the feeling of being there to look at it and to capture the moment. The feeling of walking through air — fresh air. The sound of stepping on the leaves under the skeleton of the tree.

To feel

Like it is a dream . . .

but it's real life . . .

Part Two:

Triangular shapes
different colors shining bright
the tall buildings
and the thin towers
creating a forest

Pink lights with the blue sky

Lovely to look at.
Not enough to look at for too long.

Why can I not feel anything?
Why must I just feel it's bright?
Why can't I fall into a feeling of the view?

Part Three:

Do the two views overlap and blend together or do
the two views keep their secrets? Are the two views
miles apart though they look so close? I wonder if
the two views have beauty together. I wonder if they
create a feeling together.

The struggle in this material is all too evident. The writer is carrying on a dialogue with herself based on her observations of a specific stimulus and including her reflections on subsequent feelings about that stimulus. The length and complexity of this draft, the mixture of styles, and the many unanswered questions continued to confuse and unsettle the writer. Since she found herself locked in the cycle of her own reflection, she took the subsequent poem/discourse to another peer for advice. The peer replied that the separate parts of the poem seemed as though they should belong to the same part and that the two different styles in the piece were confusing and hard to follow.

At that point, the writer took all the drafts and an account of the process and the conferences to the teacher and asked for an adult perspective. The teacher suggested that she place the picture and all the drafts side by side and, keeping her peer readers' responses in mind, attempt to isolate those images and feelings that she had first found so powerful and evocative. The poem that finally resulted can only be judged by her declared satisfaction that she had said what she had set out to say and her sense that her readers now responded as she hoped they would.

Final draft

> *Two Views in One Picture*
>
> *Black tree*
> *the dust*
> *and the moon overlapping*
> *shining like gold*
> *drowning in the color of the huge sky*
>
> *Triangular shapes*
> *different colors churning light*
> *the tall buildings*
> *and their towers*
> *creating a forest*
>
> *Mariam D. (age 13)*

(Ed. note: Mariam has since had an anthology of her poetry published. "Epigram on Abu (Father)", see page 35, was included.)

For the teacher, this kind of process presents a number of problems:

- how to keep track of who was involved, when, for how long, and for what reasons;
- how to encourage students to become involved in this kind of collaboration and help them develop a sense of their individual roles and responsibilities;
- how to ensure that the evaluation system rewards students who become involved in collaborative activities.

Tracking, the simplest aspect to monitor, follows two aspects of the collaborative process. A student confers with a peer about the peer's writing and a student asks a peer to confer about his/her own writing. Both aspects need to be tracked and rewarded. The following instruments are completed by the students themselves and retained in the writing folder. Both can be referred to by the teacher when marking the writing folder. In the writing folder marks summary sheet on page 56, both types of conferences are rewarded.

This first instrument keeps track of conferences about other people's writing. Some teachers have found it useful to glue or staple this sheet to the back of the writing folder contents sheet described on page 57. Students track with whom they conferred, when, for how long, and for what purpose. Over time, a full profile evolves of the extent and pattern of each student's collaboration with others.

The second instrument is filled out by the student writer for a specific piece of writing. This sheet records who was involved in the conference, what they were discussing, and the results of their collaboration. When stapled to the various drafts of a particular piece of writing, it fleshes out the record of that specific process. If a teacher felt it would supply a more complete picture of the process, a similar record sheet could be constructed for teacher conferences regarding specific pieces of writing.

The most important feature of this type of collaboration is what's actually being done in the conferences. Filling out record sheets such as these is an empty task if the conferences themselves are not fulfilling a student writer's needs. The conference requires participation from both the writer and the responder to keep it relevant. Depending on the individual student and the needs of the piece of writing, a revision conference might include two, three or, occasionally, four or more responders. Most conferences are best handled and seem most productive, especially with relatively inexperienced writers, when only one or two responders are present.

At the outset, the writer should try to direct the responder in some specific way. Rather than asking what's good about the piece or how the responder would change it, the writer needs to draw attention to whatever he or she is grappling with in the writing or feeling uneasy about. As well, if the writer reads the material aloud, strengths and weaknesses are sometimes more easily apprehended by the conference parties, including the writer. The responders are trying to give the writer a first-hand glimpse into how a reader reacts to the material rather than attempting to fix or improve it. The writer is trying to focus this personal reaction. The following guideline for students illustrates how this dynamic can be constructed.

Peer-Conference Record Sheet

Name: _____

Please complete the details below each time you confer about someone else's writing.

Peer's Name	Conference Type		Conference Length (min.)	Date
	Revision	Editing		

Peer-Conference Record Sheet (Writing)

Writer's Name: _____ Class: _____

Response Partner(s): _____

_____

_____

Date: _____

Title: _____

Type: [_____] non-fiction narrative   [_____] fictional narrative

[_____] poetry   [_____] review

[_____] essay   [_____] report

[_____] other (explain)

Stage: exploratory [_____]   draft # [_____]   polished [_____]

Comments/Suggestions/Questions from the Conference: _____

_____

_____

_____

Decision: file [_____]   continue drafting [_____]   publish [_____]

other _____

Guideline for Students

Peer-Revision Conference

As you discuss a piece of writing, keep in mind that both the reader and the writer have certain responsibilities in the revision process. The following questions highlight those responsibilities.

The Reader	The Writer
What, specifically, has the writer asked you to help with?	What have you asked your reader to do?
How did you respond to the material? What happened in your mind as you read? What aspects intrigued or attracted you?	What impact did the material have? How does this reaction compare with the impact you expected?
What, if anything, confused you as you read? What ideas or events were unclear? What, if anything, was left out or seemed out of place?	What will you have to take out, put in, change, or rearrange?
How did you respond to the opening and closing, to the development of ideas, or to the pace? What people or events did you want to know more about?	How can the reader help you further? What more do you want to know?

The Writing Folder

A. Final Proofreading
B. Marking Checklist

(Please complete sections A and B before handing in material for marking.)

A. Final Proofreading

Author's Name: _____

Title: _____

Type of Writing: _____

Proofreaders: (1) _____ (2) _____

Date Proofreading Completed: _____

B. Marking Checklist

I have included the following materials with my writing:
(Please mark each completed stage with a check mark.)

1. All drafts in chronological order ☐

2. All peer-conference sheets ☐

3. All teacher-conference sheets (if any) ☐

4. A marking sheet with self- and peer-
   evaluation completed ☐

By employing a clear structure defining revision strategies and rewarding revision by the author as well as peer-revision conferences and adult-revision conferences, teachers help students identify the difference between revision and editing. Students are often confused about the role of editing in the writing process, since many teachers have traditionally identified usage errors so prominently in their marking and penalized the writer accordingly. Depending on the student's age and familiarity with the writing process, teachers may find that building understanding and trust in this area takes time.

The checklist reinforces the concept that systematic editing is a later stage in the writing process. As such, it is meant only for pieces that are to be published or that are to be submitted for formal summative marking. The other important message is that peer or adult collaboration at the proofreading stage is not only allowed but actually encouraged. This message is often reinforced by teachers who help students proofread copy before it's handed in or suggest that, as well as classroom peers, students consider enlisting older brothers and sisters, parents, or other family members as proofreaders.

This process reflects the assistance given to professional writers by their editors at this stage in the writing process. It also introduces students to an active, meaningful context for focusing on the surface features of their writing without deadening their enthusiasm for the writing itself. This completed checklist along with all drafts (or enough representative drafts), conference sheets, and marks sheets are handed in when a piece of writing is submitted for publishing or formal summative marking.

Marking narrative and exposition

Formative evaluation is the ongoing assessment of student progress aimed almost exclusively at assisting students in their learning and at improving the educational experience. Such evaluation is geared to an individual's needs and personal growth. Summative evaluation, on the other hand, usually employs comparative standards and judgments in order to make an overall decision (for example, any assessment made and recorded for report card purposes). For this reason, summative evaluation is always difficult. Although diagnostic and formulative evaluation are intrinsic and welcome components of the learning process, summative evaluation is often viewed as counter-productive. However, if appropriate summative criteria are articulated and communicated to students *before* the learning process and not after, as is most common, summative evaluation can actually be totally integrated into the learning process. At the least, summative evaluation should help direct and facilitate learning. (For an ideal model, see the chapter, *Evaluating Student-Written Poetry*, pages 75-86.)

At some point, like it or not, teachers have to mark and grade student writing. Whether a student's development is compared with other students' or judged in relation to a set of specific course objectives, most schools require students to undergo regular summative evaluation. To assist with this demand, the sections on the writing folder (pages 52-58) establish basic criteria for the writing process and integrate them into the evaluation system. The other half of the mark derived from the writing folder involves a summative evaluation of product — the marking and grading of individual pieces of writing. Models for marking narrative and exposition are provided on pages 71-74. The summative evaluation of student-written poetry is covered in detail in the next chapter.

In each of the three stages of the narrative model, evaluation is required by the student author, a peer, and an adult. The adult is usually the teacher. (With the consent of the student, teachers using this model sometimes send a narrative home for a parent or older brother or sister to evaluate.) Only the *adult* mark is counted for report card purposes.

Why then require student input at all? First, by applying the evaluation criteria to their own writing, students view the characteristics of effective writing from a different perspective, a process which helps them to internalize those criteria. By evaluating the writing of their peers, students widen those experiences and apply what they have learned to their own writing. Since students develop the objectivity, confidence, and skills required for self- and peer-evaluation over time and after a number of different applications, this process allows students many opportunities to develop the essential attitudes and skills.

As well, even though the student mark is not directly counted, the student can establish a case for a particular piece of writing and direct the adult to the material's outstanding features. In the same way, the two student perspectives act as a kind of check and balance for the adult evaluator. Ideally, in general-impression marking, the same piece of writing could be evaluated by at least two and usually three different teachers, but the marking load usually prohibits this kind of 'luxury'. Student input approximates this outside assistance. A comparison of the three perspectives also provides a useful starting point in teacher/student conferences.

Writing folder marks sheets

In Part A of the marks sheet, the material is read for general impression only and a letter grading applied. The work itself is never marked for surface errors or defaced in any way. A poor application of editing procedures can be brought to the student author's attention later in the marking process. This approach ensures that editing and proofreading remain the responsibility of the student and also dramatically reduces the time a teacher needs to spend on summative evaluation.

In Part B, the comments reflect a reader's response to the content and theme. As well as preferred events or images, the reader might also mention any personal identification with the piece or areas of confusion or uncertainty. Signatures are applied to personalize and formalize the process.

Part C allows the evaluators to reflect on the various characteristics of the writing and attempt to explain how the general impression was formed. This checklist also acts as a guideline for the author if further revision is contemplated. If a piece is checked as needing additional editing or proofreading, the teacher can discuss with the student author how to make his or her approach more effective. Implicit, as well, is the understanding that the piece can be reworked, resubmitted, and marked again.

When students submit a piece for marking they are required to include all significant drafts in order: peer-conference record sheet (see page 64), the final proofreading and marking checklist (see page 67), and the marks sheet with the self- and peer-categories completed (see page 65). Stapling or clipping the package together keeps the material organized and manageable.

The process for marking exposition is exactly the same as that outlined for narrative writing. In fact, the first page of the marks sheet is identical. Obviously, however, the criteria in Part C reflect the distinctive features of expository writing.

The Writing Folder

Marks Sheet for Narrative Writing

Name: _____ Date: _____

Title: _____

A. General Impression (e.g., A, B, C)

Self [   ]   Peer [   ]   Adult [   ]

B. Comments

Self: _____

_____

_____

Peer: _____

_____

_____

Adult: _____

_____

_____

Signatures   Student: _____

Peer: _____

Adult: _____

(Please go on to Part C on the next page.)

Marks Sheet for Narrative Writing (cont'd)

C. Checking Specific Characteristics   (Please circle the appropriate letter.)

V = Very Effective   E = Effective   N = Needs Further Revision

	Self	Peer	Adult
Coherence smooth flow; sentences linked; nothing left out or out of place	V E N	V E N	V E N
Style impact of opening and closing; development of ideas	V E N	V E N	V E N
Language vivid, colorful, apt, and varied use of words, phrases, and images	V E N	V E N	V E N
Editing Proofreading spelling, punctuation, other usage — level of conventional use	V E N	V E N	V E N

The Writing Folder

Marks Sheet for Expository Writing

Name: _____ Date: _____

Title: _____

A. General Impression (e.g., A, B, C)

Self [   ]   Peer [   ]   Adult [   ]

B. Comments

Self: _____

_____

_____

Peer: _____

_____

_____

Adult: _____

_____

_____

Signatures   Student: _____

Peer: _____

Adult: _____

(Please go on to Part C on the next page.)

Marks Sheet for Expository Writing (cont'd)

C. Checking Specific Characteristics (Please circle the appropriate letter.)

V = Very Effective   E = Effective   N = Needs Further Revision

	Self	Peer	Adult
Opening Section introduces theme of essay; gets you "hooked"; leads you on	V E N	V E N	V E N
Argument each point leads on to the next; points make sense; persuasive	V E N	V E N	V E N
Coherence smooth flow; sentences linked; nothing left out or out of place	V E N	V E N	V E N
Closing Section wraps it up; brings all points together; brings argument to a close	V E N	V E N	V E N
Language vivid, colorful, apt, and varied use of words, phrases, and images	V E N	V E N	V E N
Editing Proofreading spelling, punctuation, other usage — level of conventional use	V E N	V E N	V E N

4 * Evaluating student-written poetry (a special case)

Whenever the question of evaluating and marking student-written poetry comes up, teachers usually respond in one of two ways. They admit that they have no idea how to go about it or they reply that even if they could, they wouldn't want to. Since poetry is regarded as somehow different from other forms of writing, it seems to have slipped into a peculiar, almost sacrosanct, niche in the classroom writing program. Part of this problem arises from an uneasiness with establishing criteria for the writing of poetry. While most teachers can articulate the criteria for student-written narratives and essays, and, therefore, can evaluate them, they don't seem to be willing to do the same for poetry.

Poetry's 'untouchable' status

Admittedly, both teachers and students take great delight in exploring the myriad forms of poetry from rhyme to haiku to free verse. But, while the shape or convention is taught, the process and subsequent product are regarded as too ephemeral or subjective to be marked. Evaluation would somehow mar or interfere with the message of the poem. Surely this is a double standard. Since poetry is presented as a kind of personal, private statement one shares with intimates, students start to believe that people write poetry for themselves and prose for others. Rather than protecting the genre by treating it differently, this insistence on a mystical, totally personal, and untouchable status for poetry effectively removes it from the mainstream of classroom evaluation practice.

What happens, of course, is that the writing of poetry becomes a kind of curiosity or 'breather' indulged by both students and teachers between the serious tasks of learning to write. How could it be otherwise? Students understand that marks are central to the school's value system. While students appreciate being released from the pressure of marks to revel in the freedom of poetry, they also understand its limitations in the classroom setting. For poetry to take its legitimate and central role in our struggle to make sense of and cope with our world, it must be valued in the only currency that counts in the school system — marks! In fact, some kind of valid evaluation process for poetry is desperately needed.

Setting the stage

A technique for evaluating student-written poetry in schools without disturbing the author's autonomy would require a process that included self, peer, and adult input but placed the onus for summative evaluation on the student author. The criteria for success would have to be clearly spelled out and directly related to the author's reasons for writing the poem. Such a process is not only possible but actually inevitable in a writing-process environment. Although the description of this technique may appear a little awkward, using it is simple — as long as students have had the proper introductory experiences. The key to this approach lies in the much-maligned term 'ownership'. The first stage involves students in taking control of their poetry reading before they are asked to accept responsibility for evaluating their poetry writing.

The time-honored advice to read aloud to students as much poetry as possible is still the logical and essential starting point. The next step is finding some way of assisting students to interact with, 'pick away at', and personally respond to the poetry they hear and read. Cooperative, small-group discussions provide the vehicle. One approach to using small-group discussions to allow students to unlock poetry for themselves is described by Patrick Dias and Michael Hayhoe in *Developing Response to Poetry*.

Briefly, they recommend that students be divided into small groups and presented with a poem to discuss without teacher guidance or interference. Although the opening of the discussion is rigidly prescribed, students are not directed in any other way after they start. Each student has a copy of the poem. One student reads the poem aloud to the group. One by one, in turn and without discussion, the students say something about the poem. This first reaction might be an emotional response, a question, an allusion to a particularly striking phrase or image, or a connection made with another poem. When everyone in the small group has had a chance to speak (and all responses are accepted as valid), the students begin to interact spontaneously, responding and reacting to each other's thoughts as well as to the material. If they reach a dead-end or if the discussion becomes deadlocked, one student is asked to read the poem aloud again and restart the discussion. When students ask questions of the teacher, they are turned back to the poem and instructed to read aloud the section under discussion or to move on to another section. Eventually, the small groups are asked to report to the large group on the course of their discussions and, in their reporting, to build on the previous group's report.

The benefits of this type of approach increase with practice. A number of sessions are required before students can build the confidence and self-reliance necessary to search for and find their own meanings. Nevertheless, even from the first exploratory session, students begin to realize that if answers or resolutions are going to be found, they have to do the finding themselves. They also begin to appreciate that the reading of poetry is an inherent search for meaning. The other side of the coin, of course, is that the writing of poetry is also an inherent search for meaning.

Starting the process

With a variety of listening and discussion experiences behind them and a renewed sense of their own ability to make valid judgments, students will be ready to focus their analytical and reflective skills on their own poetry as well as the poetry of their peers. When students are ready to have poems evaluated in a *summative* way, they take them through a four-part process. Prior to this stage, they can engage in as many peer- and adult-revision conferences as they like. Whatever assistance or advice they need and whatever reshaping, crafting, or polishing they do should all precede this evaluation process.

The evaluation has four components, each of which is completed in the following sequence:

1. Step One by the student author.

2. Step Two by one or more peers.

3. Step Three by the teacher or other adult.

4. Step Four by the student author.

Poetry Evaluation Process: Step One

In this first step, students are asked to reflect on and articulate their intentions in creating a specific poem and to predict reader reaction and response to both the meaning and the form of the poem.

A. Initial Self-Evaluation

Author's Name: _____

Title of Poem: _____

What aspects of your poem do you think your readers will enjoy or be affected or intrigued by? Please talk about your poem in your own way. The following questions are only suggestions and do not need to be answered.

The Meaning

How do you want your readers to respond to this poem? What will the poem make them think about? How will the poem involve them? What questions or comments will the poem stir up?

_____

_____

_____

_____

_____

The Form

What aspects of your use of language do you want your readers to appreciate or enjoy (for example, vivid, colorful, apt use of words, phrases, images; effective placement of words, phrases, lines on page; special forms such as haiku, optic, rhyming poems)?

_____

_____

_____

Poetry Evaluation Process: Step Two

In the second step, one or more peers are asked to declare their own personal reactions to the poem and to reflect on those aspects of form and meaning that, for whatever reasons, seem to have particular relevance.

B. Peer Evaluation

Peer Evaluator's Name: _____

Author's Name: _____

Title of Poem: _____

What aspects of the poem did you enjoy and how did the poem affect or intrigue you? Please talk about the poem in your own way. The following questions are only suggestions and do not need to be answered.

The Meaning

How did you respond to this poem? What did you start thinking about? How did the poem involve you? What questions or comments do you have?

_____

_____

_____

_____

_____

The Form

What aspects of the language of the poem did you particularly appreciate or enjoy (e.g., vivid, colorful, apt use of words, phrases, images; effective placement of words, phrases, lines on page; special forms such as haiku, optic, rhyming poems)?

_____

_____

_____

_____

Poetry Evaluation Process: Step Three

In the third step, the teacher or other adult responds in the same way as the author's peers, providing the student author with at least two persepctives.

C. Teacher/Adult Evaluation

Evaluator's Name: _____

Author's Name: _____

Title of Poem: _____

What aspects of the poem did you enjoy and how did the poem affect or intrigue you? The following questions are only suggestions and do not need to be answered.

The Meaning

How did you respond to this poem? What did you start thinking about? How did the poem involve you? What questions or comments do you have?

_____

_____

_____

_____

_____

The Form

What aspects of the language of the poem did you particularly appreciate or enjoy (e.g., vivid, colorful, apt use of words, phrases, images; effective placement of words, phrases, lines on page; special forms such as haiku, optic, rhyming poems)?

_____

_____

_____

_____

Poetry Evaluation Process: Step Four

In this final stage, the student author reviews all the sheets and reflects on how successful he or she was in reaching and affecting readers. The author's intentions and expectations are compared with the outcome as represented by the peer and adult 'feedback' sheets (steps two and three).

D. Final Self-Evaluation

To what extent were your readers affected by the poem *as you had intended*? What surprised, pleased, or disappointed you about the way your poem was received?

_____

_____

_____

_____

_____

_____

_____

Overall, how would you rate your success in reaching and affecting your audience as you intended with this poem? Please circle the most appropriate letter.

C. Successful   B. Quite Successful   A. Most Successful

Date: _____   Author's Signature: _____

The first two steps are under the control of the student author. The actual marks are assigned in the last step. Peers take an integral part in this process and other adults, such as parents or teachers, can substitute in the process for the classroom teacher.

What about marks?

For summative purposes, the C, B, A designations on the 'successful' to 'most successful' range can each be accepted at face value as a letter grading and, if necessary, can be translated into an equivalent and appropriate numerical rating. In other words, a poem rated as 'most successful' is rated as an "A" poem and given whatever percentage an "A" usually receives in that classroom's evaluation system.

The key to this process is the identification of the reward with the success the author achieved in reaching his or her audience *as intended*. Writing is a purposeful activity. If marks are to be assigned, they should mirror the degree of success in achieving the purpose for that writing. In this particular process for evaluating student-written poetry, goals are identified, outcomes are analyzed, and the effectiveness of the poem evaluated by the person who wrote it. In addition, the intrinsic link between process and product is reflected in the evaluation process. However awkward and cumbersome the process may appear, it does work and it does place the responsibility for evaluation directly on the students — where it belongs.

Ownership and integrity

Some people might ask what keeps students from inflating their own marks once they realize that the marks are under their control. Certainly, a teacher can choose to confer with a student individually and review the results of the evaluation process. At that time, the student can be asked to justify the grading. Through the review process, students may want to adjust marks up or down or just take an adjusted perspective into their next round of evaluation of new material. In actual practice, however, students almost invariably accept their newfound and real responsibilities with great seriousness and personal commitment. Any differences that occur are differences of opinion or understanding, not differences in integrity. When students truly write to make sense of and cope with their world, a logical and inevitable outcome of that process has to be an understanding of and a commitment to their personal integrity.

Poetry evaluation process-student sample

In the following evaluations of "Cecelia's Rainbow" (page 38), the student author conveys her understanding of the writing process and her personal commitment to the poem. Notice that all three respondents (author, peer, and adult) focus on the poetic experience itself and become caught up in a celebration of the poem's impact. The concluding self-evaluation reveals the author's thrill at having touched an audience as she had intended.

Poetry Evaluation Process: Step One

In this first step, students are asked to reflect on and articulate their intentions in creating a specific poem and to predict reader reaction and response to both the meaning and the form of the poem.

A. Initial Self-Evaluation

Author's Name: _____*Karen C.*_____

Title of Poem: _____*"Cecelia's Rainbow"*_____

What aspects of your poem do you think your readers will enjoy or be affected or intrigued by? Please talk about your poem in your own way. The following questions are only suggestions and do not need to be answered.

The Meaning

How do you want your readers to respond to this poem? What will the poem make them think about? How will the poem involve them? What questions or comments will the poem stir up?

I want readers to feel attached to this poem. I hope the poem

will rouse their childhood memories. It might involve them in a

---

similar situation from when they were young. They might wonder

whether or not this was a real experience.

The Form

What aspects of your use of language do you want your readers to appreciate or enjoy (for example, vivid, colorful, apt use of words, phrases, images; effective placement of words, phrases, lines on page; special forms such as haiku, optic, rhyming poems)?

I want my readers to enjoy the childlike atmosphere of the

poem. I think the rhyme and the rhythm will remind them of

children's poetry from their past.

Poetry Evaluation Process: Step Two

B. Peer Evaluation

The Meaning

I think the poem created a clear picture of what was going on in

the story. The characters seemed real and talked and acted like

real people. It was really touching.

The Form

We mostly hear poems that only rhyme a little if they do at all

and this had a real rhyme to it. It was fun to read and the

words seemed to be just right. The poem had a lot of color to it

and seemed like a picture or a movie.

Poetry Evaluation Process: Step Three

C. Teacher/Adult Evaluation

The Meaning

What a joy to see the world once again through a child's eyes!
All at once, I was able to appreciate the wonder and joy that
the natural, spontaneous world brings!

The Form

The character of the child shines through. The images are apt
and appealing. The rhymes are clever and appropriate and most
enjoyable.

Poetry Evaluation Process: Step Four

D. Final Self-Evaluation

I was very pleased that my readers enjoyed seeing things
through a child's eyes the way I hoped they would. I wasn't at
all disappointed in the way it was received. I think this poem
was most successful.

5 * Getting back on the tracks: an implementation review

What's in a name?

What's new about the drafting process?

The push to publish or the book-of-the-day club

Buddy authoring, again?

Deus ex machina: the computer takes over

Writing folder or miscellaneous file?

The Writing Process?
Writing as Process?
Process Writing?
The Writing Folder?

Which of these is the 'buzz' phrase in your school? Has everyone settled on a common meaning? Better yet, how does it translate into classroom practice? Although all of these terms are supposed to denote the new, process-oriented approach to writing in schools, what that approach actually signifies for classroom programs is often confusing and difficult to pin down.

What's in a name?

How many of the following explanations have you heard? *The 'writing process' approach means that . . .*

. . . *students 'see' themselves as authors.*
. . . *the drafting process is mirrored in and facilitated by a writing folder.*
. . . *students write and publish for actual audiences.*
. . . *student authors are 'empowered'.*
. . . *writing is integrated into a 'whole language' process or program.*

The last statement, of course, raises the equally intriguing question, *Heard any good definitions of 'whole language' lately?*

What is clear is that, as a process orientation toward writing moved out of the formative stages of hypothesis, investigation, and experimentation and into the mainstream of the classroom, diversity flourished. Now that schools have weathered the initial surge of process implementation, the time is ripe to review these classroom writing programs, identify the strengths of the various interpretations and approaches, and offer a few words of caution. (The concept strands described in the appendix are intended to direct teachers back to the areas of this book most likely to help them in their ongoing implementation.)

Over the past few years, as more and more educators have tried to translate current research on the subject of writing into classroom practice, the tidal wave of words has had several side effects. Since the writing process concept had attracted so much interest and had gained general acceptance, school administrators and subject consultants rushed to jump on the bandwagon, dragging their teachers in tow, of course. Naturally enough, after listening to all the talk, most of the 'enlisted' teachers co-opted the definition of the writing process that best suited their own established programs and specific school context. Whether they were English teachers directing a writer's workshop course for senior students, history specialists picking up an English class at the intermediate level, or elementary teachers with responsibility for the entire curriculum, they were expected to implement the writing process approach as quickly as possible. At the elementary and intermediate levels especially, they simply incorporated into their programs particular characteristics of the new wave, such as composing and drafting by computer or establishing a school publishing centre.

What's wrong with that? Unfortunately, in the rush to make writing programs look the part, the form of the process often undercut and derailed the essential heart of the program. The publishing of student writing, for example, does not necessarily ensure a valid writing process; neither do transcribing and drafting on a computer. A brief sortie through the minefield of popular practice will illuminate a few basic principles and underscore what will ensure a valid writing process. The concept of drafting, for example, is often used synonymously with the writing process.

What's new about the drafting process?

Almost nothing. When teachers try to articulate what the writing process actually entails, however, they invariably mention drafting. To most teachers, drafting denotes the process by which students write in rough, revise this writing through an unspecified number of stages, often with peer assistance, edit and proofread, again collaboratively, and hand in a 'clean', polished product for publication and/or summative evaluation (marking).

The drafting process today often includes a few new wrinkles, including valuable peer cooperation which, in former years, was usually missing. (See chapter 3, *The Writing Process Toolkit,* pages 49-74, for tips on stimulating and keeping track of student collaboration.) As well, mindful of the need for student ownership, teachers seem far more respectful of their students' written work, especially the final product, and are less likely to bleed red corrections and comments all over the pages. Yet, even in this form, the drafting procedure still superimposes an external, linear structure on to what should be a personal, recursive process.

In actual practice, given the realities of classroom management, the drafting process often becomes truncated and fossilized. Timetable constraints, limited access to computers, the need for marks for report card purposes, and fragmented English/language arts programs are just some of the factors that tend to abberate the intended approach. Often, everything students write is taken through the process. Distinctions between revision and editing are blurred and, to save time, blended into a single stage; the rough copy is revised and edited and, from it, a final or simply a polished copy is prepared.

Although some form of peer-editing is often grafted on the process, this approach to drafting seems little changed from the rough-copy/final-copy sequence teachers have traditionally demanded from their students. Small wonder, then, that many teachers question what all the fuss is about, unless, of course, their definition of the writing process revolves around the publication of student writing.

The push to publish or the book-of-the-day club

Current changes in the approach to *reading* instruction have greatly influenced changes in the approach to writing.

'Good' readers — research

When researchers like Frank Smith began to examine how effective readers read in order to find a model that less effective readers could emulate, the teaching of reading was revolutionized, as the regular reprinting of Smith's *Understanding Reading* attests. Until then, the accepted way to remediate ineffective reading had been decidedly behavioristic. After isolating a series of discrete reading skills and arranging them in scope and sequence, for example, a teacher diagnosed faulty skills and drilled and tested to remediate or eliminate them. This approach was supported by a vast reservoir of specially designed (and, often, expensive) 'skill-and-drill' learning material packages.

When researchers articulated the actual skills that separated a 'good' reader from a 'poor' one, however, teachers were then able to develop new directions for classroom practice. In an effective program, teachers now allowed all students, regardless of reading ability, to self-select reading material, gave them daily time to read independently, frequently read aloud to them, and invited and valued personal response to a variety of reading experiences.

'Good' writers — research

With the success of programs based on research into how 'good' readers read, related research into how 'good' writers write promised even greater benefits. Unlike reading, writing led to an observable product. As well, the active processes of writing were also more easily observed. Researcher/writers and teacher/writers began to reflect on their own writing processes, to compare them with the observable behaviors of students writing in classrooms, and to determine how the differences affected classroom programs. Since the publication of *Writing: Teachers and Children at Work*, Donald Graves, for example, has had such a profound influence on writing in classrooms that teachers universally are acquainted with the "Graves Model" of implementing the writing process (even though Graves himself disowns the kind of rigid approach most advocates of the "Graves Model" attempt). Over the last few years, Nancy Atwell's account of her classroom experiences implementing a writer's workshop approach, *In the Middle*, has had enormous impact on writing programs in the intermediate years.

In traditional programs, the time devoted to 'composition' was relegated to the slot left over after reading/literature, spelling, and so-called 'grammar' components had been satisfied. From the students' point of view, the major goal in those 'composition' classes seemed to be learning how to produce a product with as few surface errors as possible. The damage done by this debilitating, behavioristic, and fragmented approach to writing is well documented.

Publishing

One of the most obvious differences in many of the new approaches and the one most easily introduced into the classroom involved publishing. With the addition of self-selection of writing topics, a daily time to write, and a drafting process with publication as its goal, classroom writing programs were revolutionized. Publishing centres sprang up in schools everywhere. Rather than directing all their writing to the teacher as reader/evaluator, students now wrote for 'real' audiences, such as their peers, and were gratified and stimulated by the expanded audience that publishing gave them. For student authors and student reading audience alike, the reading/writing connection seemed firmly and meaningfully joined. Meanwhile, teachers and parents pointed to the tangible output as proof-positive that the writing process flourished.

Ironically, as publishing centres gained the spotlight, the writing process became confused with and overshadowed by product. Publishing does require some kind of drafting process. As already noted, drafting is not particularly new. Neither is the publishing of student-written material, although the sheer amount of it being done today is unprecedented. What is new is the number of students who speak knowingly of 'writer's block'. The joy a Grade 2 child experiences seeing his/her words in print for the first time is never as spontaneous or as full-fledged or as deeply felt the second or sixth or tenth time the process occurs. What about the child who is caught up in the 'publish or perish' syndrome for the second or sixth or tenth *year*?

The analogy between professional writers writing in an adult context and student writers writing in a classroom context is only partially valid. The differences are as important as the similarities. Most adult authors publish because they feel they have something of worth to share with as large an audience as possible. Other reasons may include writing for prestige, job security, or money. Such distinctions have been ignored in the transfer of the publishing process to schools, along with the inherent right of authors *not* to publish, if they see fit.

The 'joy' of writing

Whatever else teachers do with the publishing phenomenon in their schools, they should be honest about the so-called 'joy' of writing. Everyone may or may not have a novel 'inside' to be written and published for all the world to enjoy. What non-writers don't really appreciate, in their admiration of those who do get their work in print, is how truly tedious, difficult, and downright daunting writing can be. Whether a novelist, a newspaper columnist, or an executive secretary with responsibility for the company newsletter, writers know the dread and drudgery of filling up the page. Is it any wonder that so much of the world's great literature has been produced by haunted, driven, and, often, emotionally tortured individuals? They write not out of choice but out of need; the motivation is intrinsic rather than extrinsic. (Chapter 2, *In the World of the Classroom*, explored the implications of this distinction for schools.)

Buddy authoring, again?

The connection between the new direction in reading instruction and the increased emphasis on student publishing has produced a new genre of student writing in schools. For years, teachers have paired older students with younger students for 'buddy reading' periods. Usually, the older student read aloud a picture book of interest to the younger student. Together, they discussed the various characteristics and enjoyable aspects of the book. The older student had an authentic reason for reading aloud and the younger student derived the benefits of being read to, especially when the interest factor could be individualized. Both benefitted from the opportunities for interaction and reflection generated by the print experience.

Collaborating on picture book projects

Taking the concept one step further, teachers recognized the potential in these pairings for authenticating and individualizing the author/audience link in a powerful new way. After a number of these readaloud experiences, the 'buddies' were encouraged to confer on the theme and plot of a new picture book, conceived jointly and, later, carried out by the older partner. Sometimes, when the pairing crossed division levels, such as when a secondary school creative writing class was paired with an elementary school class, both the process and the product became quite complex and sophisticated. Story updating and revision conferences were arranged for the partners at various stages of the composing process, peer-revision and peer-editing components were included, contracts were made with accomplished student illustrators, and visits by professional authors and storytellers were incorporated. When a publishing party was added at the conclusion of the unit, at which the new picture books were unveiled and read to the younger 'buddies', the process truly came full circle.

Benefits and cautions

For student authors, creating a picture book offered a number of compelling bonuses. Through their own early childhood reading experiences, they intrinsically understood the models on which such writing was based. Since the language was kept relatively simple for the designated audience and the structure of these specialized narratives was easily comprehended, students were better able to assess and manage this kind of writing than they were the narratives they wrote for peers or adults. Illustrating the text added a familiar and enjoyable component usually neglected beyond the junior grades and the cross-grade interaction and collaboration allowed students to personalize and focus their work.

Unfortunately, a good idea at one level is quite often a good idea at another level. From senior secondary writing classes to intermediate English classes to junior language arts programs, teachers everywhere began to incorporate some kind of 'buddy authoring' and picture book project into their programs. Predictably, after a few years, teachers in the intermediate grades started hearing, "Do we have to do a picture book again?" Beyond the obvious danger of familiarity, the repetition of this approach had clearly produced a mixed blessing. Students had become quite adept at this particular process and the product became increasingly more sophisticated. On the other hand, the widespread use of this approach underlined how easily specific tactics in a process orientation could be mistaken for the process itself. Regardless of a teacher's philosophy or methodology, the strategy was easily co-opted and grafted on almost any language program. Rather than advancing the cause and understanding of the writing process, the use of this technique demontrated how an engaging, if limited, variation on the classroom publishing phenomenon could very quickly become institutionalized and then fossilized.

Deus ex machina: the computer takes over

Word processing presents the teacher with a vehicle tailor-made for the writing process. Text is manipulated quickly and efficiently and the need for mindless recopying and the myriad problems associated with handwriting are totally eliminated. With desk-top publishing only a keyboard away, students truly control every stage their writing goes through. Understandably, many teachers point to the computer lab when they want to define the writing process.

Composing or merely transcribing

What is actually happening at these consoles in classrooms and school computer labs everywhere, of course, makes it clear that this potential remains largely untapped. The first obstacle to overcome is finding enough 'time on task'. Since a school can afford only so many computers, on-line time is at a premium, especially since word processing is only one of many uses for computers in the school curriculum. Whether a school tries to place one or two computers in each classroom or sets up a central computer lab, each student usually winds up with only a few minutes per week for word processing. Actual observation of students working at computers reveals that they spend most of their computer time transcribing rather than composing. And why not? With so little actual time available at the keyboard, using that time for transcribing a late, handwritten draft makes perfect sense.

Help from home?

Even at home, students spend surprisingly little time at word processing. One would expect the growing number of home computers would be easing the problem of limited access at school, but the technology of computer home video games has kept pace with the new generation of word processors with the result that the sophisticated lure of video games continues to keep many students from fully exploring the potential of writing by computer. When the interest is there, availability often isn't. Since parents have been quick to pick up on the versatility of the home computer, students often find access at home as limited as access at school. Besides, if home and school do not use the same systems, incompatability from computer to computer creates more frustration. Students may keep one data disk at school for the school computer and one at home for the home computer, and be unable to interchange them.

Outdated equipment

If anything, schools are falling behind homes in taking advantage of the potential in the newer technology. Quite often, students have superior hardware and software at home. With school funding always a problem, once schools have invested in computers, they are reluctant to replace or upgrade them. While some schools are able to afford the new generation of computers and software with expanded potential and simplified operation, most schools are sputtering along with outdated equipment. This older equipment has a limited capacity and the word-processing programs make the manipulation of text an awkward and complicated process.

Keyboarding skills?

Even with the new generation of computers, many students utilize the 'hunt and peck' system of keyboarding. When and how to teach keyboarding skills remain controversial issues. Typing manuals used at the secondary school level provide the most common model of instruction. Unfortunately, 'time on task' seems to be the essential requirement in the teaching of keyboarding. Since no one seems to have found a way to integrate the amount of sheer practice time required to develop mechanical skill with the kind of meaningful writing students need to do, the mind-dulling routine associated with typing classes remains to haunt the computer age.

Even when special software is available, formal instruction in keyboarding is left to the secondary level for those students heading for a computer or business orientation. For younger students, even when the necessary physical dexterity is present, the question of whether or not an emphasis too early on keyboarding practice actually interferes with the development of vital affective attitudes toward writing remains unresolved. Apart from a basic introduction to the function of special keys and access to keyboarding software, most students are left with little or no instruction in, motivation toward, or time to practise keyboarding.

Keyboarding partners

Teachers try in different ways to minimize the shortcomings associated with limited access. A common strategy, pairing students at each terminal, would appear to be an obvious means of increasing keyboard time, but in actual practice it delivers mixed outcomes. Interaction for revising and editing may be facilitated, but personal reflection and expression during composing is made more difficult. The chances are quite good that a student will wind up with a well-edited version of a mediocre narrative.

"Garbage in - garbage out"

If anything, the use of computers has only underscored the failure of schools to come to terms with a true process orientation toward writing. Having the 'product' in full view on the monitor and a hard copy only a simple printing command away keeps the attention firmly focused on the end point rather than on the journey. Even though text can be readily handled in a variety of ways, students continue to neglect revision in favor of editing for surface features. The spelling check, unfortunately, tends to encourage this superficial approach. In a sense, the computer screen offers a picture that is too neat and cut-and-dried for the messy business of thinking through writing. Have you ever heard computer-literate people talk about "garbage in - garbage out"? Process-oriented writers, on the other hand, always filter the 'garbage', discarding some bits, recycling others, and treasuring those few bits buried in the heart of the 'garbage' that make the search so necessary and so worthwhile.

Writing folder or miscellaneous file?

Writing folders are so much in vogue today that many teachers assume they are synonymous with the writing process. To complicate matters, teachers often use different types of writing folders for different functions, confusing 'working' writing folders with 'cumulative' writing folders.

'Working' writing folder

A 'working' writing folder is a system that organizes student writing in such a way that the recursive stages in the writing process are facilitated. Some teachers advocate one of a variety of commercially-available folders; others staple or tape together two legal-size, file folders to produce a three-pocket effect; still others continue to have their students use a notebook or loose-leaf binder.

Whatever the form of the folder, the function should be to mirror and facilitate the various stages of the writing process. Brainstorming lists, fragments, false starts, and rough drafts of all kinds should have a place in the folder. It should allow material to be worked on, placed back in the 'rough' section, when necessary, and a different piece pulled out for consideration. Some mechanism is also necessary for tracking peer- and adult-revision, editing conferences, and progress through the drafting stages. A look through such a folder at any one time would reveal material at all stages from inert, rough drafts to polished pieces ready for publication or marking.

'Cumulative' writing folder

As well as 'working' folders, many schools and even boards or districts provide 'cumulative' writing folders, one per student. As the name suggests, these folders are portfolios for student writing. Each year, a few representative, polished pieces of writing are added to the folder. Ideally, both teacher and student have input into the selection. As the portfolio grows, year by year, both student and successive teachers have a unique window into that individual's growth in writing over time and ready access to each student's finest efforts from year to year.

Again, whatever the potential of the writing folder system, in actual practice it frequently breaks down. Teachers have not always been able to structure the use of the folders to accommodate the clutter of the recursive process on the one hand and a discernible, functional organization to shape and process that clutter on the other. The folders usually degenerate into storage compartments for loose bits of paper from all subject areas.

As far as the cumulative folders are concerned, some schools find them useful, even enlightening, and maintain their use from year to year and teacher to teacher. The system breaks down when students go from one school to another and from one level to another. Even within individual schools, unless all teachers believe in their value and promote their use, they tend to disappear relatively quickly. If teachers are operating in a 'writer's workshop' context, a cumulative folder offers a wealth of diagnostic information. If they aren't, the folders become just one more, unwanted, housekeeping task. (See chapter 3, *The Writing Process Toolkit*, for a comprehensive and practical plan for revitalizing, managing, and evaluating the writing folder.)

Epilogue

Finding the 'write' balance

The writing process movement has dramatically altered how teachers approach writing in their classrooms. The popularity of some form of drafting, publishing for real audiences, word processing, or writing folders attests to the widespread belief in a process orientation. As well as exploring what happens to these principles as they move out of the academic world of hypothesis and research and into the world of the classroom, this book has also proposed a variety of practical bridges to span the two worlds. At this point, however, a few cautions need to be raised.

Finding the 'write' balance

While a process-oriented approach to writing has had many positive effects, a rigid adherence to some of the main features can produce an opposite reaction. Take the publication of student writing, for example. No educator would question the value of students writing for a real audience or having their work published. But not every student experiences the 'joy' of writing and not every writer wants his/her writing published, even the first time. (Indeed, some writing is never intended for publication.) A school-wide or class-wide emphasis on this one feature can easily upset the delicate balance between process and product and turn the writing process into a production line. Anger and frustration can also erupt when the inherent right of authors *not* to publish is ignored.

Equally unfortunate is the fact that the publishing focus, specifically, and a process orientation, in general, can obscure the many other valid and vital reasons for writing. For example, writing to record ideas, facts, or experiences for oneself, as well as for others, is an essential life skill. Even more important is the realization that writing and thinking are so closely linked that, for many people, they're interdependent. In this case, thinking through a problem or issue for oneself rather than communicating with others becomes the goal; reflection rather than publishing is the process and writing is the key.

Over the years, in publications from N.A.T.E. (National Association of Teachers of English), English educators like Douglas Barnes, Mike Torbe, and Peter Medway have ably demonstrated that language is for thinking as well as for communicating. Across the curriculum, when we are learning *through* language, that use of language can be hesitant, tentative, halting, repetitive, and recursive. The goal is understanding. As understanding is achieved and our goal becomes communication, fluency improves, but if we focus on fluency before the goal of communication is achieved, we interfere with understanding. The growing use of learning logs and response journals of all kinds acknowledges how essential a student's personal language is in learning. If surface errors or mode of expression were 'marked' in logs and journals, the benefits deriving from their use would be destroyed. Personal response can actually enhance all aspects of a whole-language program. Since this approach directs students to examine the crucial link between how they learn and what they learn, evaluation must be based on learning criteria rather than fluency criteria.

In any effective writing program, ends and means are intrinsically linked. The steps in a writing process, for example, become mindless drill when the writer has nothing to say. By the same token, if the goal is to reflect on or extend learning, the process necessarily becomes an end in itself. In either case, the imposition of the revising/editing cycle would be counter-productive. No one wants a return to the days when language was taught in a fragmented and functionless manner. On the other hand, the critical role that writing plays in thinking and learning can be reaffirmed without disrupting the benefits derived from the writing process movement. If the function of the writing determines the nature of the process, a balance among writing's various roles can be achieved. In the real world of the classroom, that balance is essential.

102

Appendices

Concept strands
Glossary
Selected and annotated bibliography

Concept strands

As teachers review their own beliefs about and approaches to the writing process, they want a few essential questions answered. The answers to these questions allow them to compare what they would like to be achieving in their writing programs with what they are actually doing. As with the recursive nature of the writing process itself, this book has no real ending. Instead, to assist teachers in their informal gap analysis and the never-ending cycle of review and implementation, the material has been organized, here, into concept strands. By following these strands, teachers can retrieve information in a specific sequence. The guiding questions and subsequent strands follow:

- What do other teachers do in their writing programs? (Practices)

- What is actually meant by the writing process? (Process)

- How is the process put into practice? (Writing Folder)

- How is the writing process evaluated? (Evaluation)

Writing practices

buddy authoring 93-95
drafting 89-90
electronic communication (by modem) 36-41
first-hand experience 32-35
'free' writing 28-31
journal writing 16-23
learning logs 23-28
poetry 76-86
publishing 90-92, 102
thinking and reflecting 103
word processing 95-97

Writing process

barriers to 41-42
basic principles 43-44
collaboration on revising and editing 58-68
collaboration, problems with 62
co-opting the definition 89
definition 42
description 8-11
language across the curriculum 103
language assessment survey 45-47
product versus process 50
risk-taking 50
start, learning where to 44-45
teacher roles 15-16

Writing folder

conference guidelines 63-66
'cumulative' 98
evaluation 54-68
marks summary sheet 56
tracking conferences 62-65
tracking contents 57-58
tracking writing activities — student sample 52-54
uses 97-99
'working' 98

Writing evaluation

diagnostic 44-47
expository marks sheets 73-74
inconsistencies 50-52
narrative writing marks sheets 71-72
poetry process 76-86
writing folder 54-58
writing folder or miscellaneous file 97-99

Glossary

The definitions in this selected glossary reflect the meanings that are used in the text.

brainstorming: generating a list of examples, ideas, or questions to illustrate, expand, or explore central idea or topic (record all ideas; no evaluating of ideas during collecting; quantity of ideas is important; encourage students to expand on each other's ideas; 'zany' ideas are welcome)

composing: the process of putting words together to form an effective message or artistic statement in speech or writing (not to be confused with **transcribing**); also referred to as 'composition'

conferencing: opportunities to discuss ideas and problems in pairs or small groups; conferences can be conducted in a variety of formats with and without the teacher

co-operative learning: a variety of small-group instructional techniques focusing on peer collaboration

cumulative writing folder: a folder containing representative pieces of a student's writing passed on to the next year's teacher, one folder per student. As material accumulates over the years, periodic 'weeding' is recommended

desk-top publishing: using the resources of the personal computer to give individuals access to the publishing process; software ranges from simple word processing programs to sophisticated publishing programs offering a variety of text and graphic capabilities

diagnostic evaluation: an aspect of formative evaluation; becoming familiar with each student's interests, abilities, preferred learning style, and learning difficulties

diary (private): an in-class record of personal observations, random jottings, and a daily record of thoughts and feelings; shared only if the student agrees; difficult to maintain over time or adapt for use in other parts of the writing program (see also **journal, log**)

editing: checking, prior to a final copy, for errors in spelling, usage, and clarity of expression (The regular use of peer- and small-group editing techniques is highly recommended.)

evaluation: determining progress toward and attainment of specific goals; assessing student progress and achievement and program effectiveness (see also **diagnostic evaluation, formative evaluation,** and **summative evaluation**)

expressive mode: includes journals, sharing personal experiences, exploratory writing, projecting into the experience of another, personal letters

fluency: the ability to speak, write, or read aloud experiences, smoothly, easily, and with clear expression of ideas

formative evaluation: the ongoing assessment of student progress aimed almost exclusively at assisting learning and at improving the educational experience; geared to an individual's needs and personal growth

holistic mark: a general-impression mark given after one reading

journal (public): a less private form of diary; is more readily shared, allows more flexibility, and is more adaptable as a teaching tool; especially useful when used to elicit personal responses to reading and issues and events under study and when the writing is used in other parts of the writing program (see also **diary, log**)

language across the curriculum: also referred to as 'learning through language across the curriculum'; an approach to the learning/teaching environment that recognizes that language is intrinsic to thinking and learning; among the basic principles is the realization that students need to 'think aloud' in their own talk or style of writing in order to fully understand concepts; during the talking and writing process, concepts are examined, analyzed, reformulated, and defined in a personal and individual manner

literacy: basically the ability to read and write; extended today to include the processing of information from all sources and systems, including electronic and microelectronic

literature: writing of high quality and significance because of a successful integration of such components as style, organization, language, and theme

log: a calendar-like record of the events of a day or a week (see also **journal, diary**)

'making meaning': the recognition that the act of processing language involves more than the communicating or recording of experience; through language we tend to construct our sense of experience by clarifying, discovering, assessing, reflecting on, resolving, and refining what we really think and feel about experience

modeling: the act of serving as an example of behavior: for example, a teacher reads during independent reading periods, displays a genuine courtesy toward others and a respect for individual differences, or demonstrates revision strategies using a piece of his or her own writing

personal response: encouraging students to begin an explication of and reflection on material with their own ideosyncratic, immediate, and spontaneous impressions, reactions, and questions where and when they arise; includes the recognition that our listening, speaking, reading, writing, viewing, and thinking processes are directed toward 'making meaning' (see **'making meaning'**, above)

personal reading: reading self-selected materials; also, reading material which may be suggested by someone else but which is so interesting and stimulating that the student becomes independently engaged by the experience

personal writing: writing about self-selected issues and events arising from an individual's daily life or interests; also, any writing that involves a student to such an extent that he/she is independently motivated to complete the experience

poetic mode: includes stories, poems, patterning from literature

process writing: see **writing as process**

pre-writing (rehearsing): activities and experiences occurring before the actual writing begins; includes talking, reading, picture-making, informal responses

publishing centre: a facility within a school for publishing student writing; often located in the school library and including such equipment as a word processor and printer, a book binder, and possibly a laminator; frequently staffed by parent volunteers or senior students (see also **desk-top publishing**)

readalouds: any material read aloud, usually by the teacher; students of all ages should be read to regularly; readalouds should comprise both fiction and non-fiction and should be drawn from a variety of genres

response journal: a notebook or folder in which students record their personal reactions to, questions about, and reflections on what they read, view, listen to, and discuss in addition to how they actually go about reading, viewing, listening, and discussing

revision: includes adding and deleting words, phrases, sentences, and even entire paragraphs, putting ideas in different order, changing ideas

risk-taking: the internalized understanding that mistakes/approximations are *good*; the freedom to experiment, extend the known, or try something new without unduly worrying about failing or being wrong

storytelling: an oral tradition in which the structure and substance of a story are learned or memorized, but not the exact words. Stories may include legend, oral lore, wonder tales, stories about how and why, epic narrative, and personal history.

summative evaluation: usually employs comparative standards and judgments in order to make an overall decision (for example, any assessment made and recorded for report card purposes)

transcribing: writing out or typing a copy; the physical act as distinguished from the creative process (see **composing**)

transactional mode: focuses on providing information; includes reports, instructions, arguments, scientific observations, business letters

usage: the customary or preferred way of using specific items of language in such areas as pronunciation, vocabulary, and syntax

whole language: a learning/teaching approach that emphasizes the integration of language 'threads' (i.e., listening, speaking, reading, writing, viewing, thinking) within the context of meaningful communication (e.g., a single writing task may engage a student in a range of discussion, composing, editing/revising, reading tasks); includes the idea of moving away from isolated, fragmented approaches, such as a regular 'grammar' period outside the context of the writing process

writer's workshop: organizing the classroom writing program to reflect and facilitate the writing process; includes such components as maintaining a writing folder, collaboration among students for composing, revising, and editing, and regular student-teacher writing conferences; frequent sharing and publishing of student writing are often important features

writing folder: a folder or notebook organized to accommodate and facilitate the various stages in the writing process; sometimes used as a synonym for writing as process (see **writing as process**)

writing as process: the recursive and blended elements of writing: pre-writing, writing, post-writing; includes writing for actual audiences other than the teacher and for purposes other than summative evaluation

Selected and annotated bibliography

The interest in writing in schools in recent years has produced a wealth of valuable and stimulating resources. The references that follow emerged as touchstones as this book developed. The list is notable for the many fine texts not mentioned.

Atwell, Nancie. *In the Middle: Writing, Reading, and Learning with Adolescents.* Portsmouth, New Hampshire: Boynton/Cook Publishers, 1987.

One teacher's personal narrative of how she worked her way through to a better understanding of how to help her students 'make meaning'; presents a real teacher with real students in a real classroom.

Barnes, Douglas. *From Communication to Curriculum.* England: Penguin, 1976.

Establishes and explores the fundamental principles of language use in classrooms; as stimulating now as when first published.

Dias, Patrick and Hayhoe, Michael. *Developing Response to Poetry.* Milton Keynes, Philadelphia: Open University Press, 1988.

Presents a compelling technique for allowing students to 'unlock' poetry in their own way through peer-discussion groups.

Graves, Donald H. *Discover Your Own Literacy.* Portsmouth, New Hampshire: Heinemann, 1990.

A vision of the classroom as a community of learners within which adults and children together investigate and develop their own literacy.

Graves, Donald H. *Writing: Teachers and Children at Work.* Portsmouth, New Hampshire: Heinemann Educational Books, 1983.

How the vision of a writing process began.

Martin, Nancy, and Medway, Peter. *From Talking to Writing*. London: Ward Lock Educational, 1977.

A short, provocative pamphlet dealing with talking and writing for 'real' purposes.

Parsons, Les. *Response Journals*. Markham, Ontario: Pembroke Publishers Limited/Portsmouth, New Hampshire: Heinemann Educational Books, Inc., 1990.

A comprehensive handbook for implementing a whole-language program based on personal response.

Spear, Karen. *Sharing Writing: Peer Response Groups in English Classes*. Portsmouth, New Hampshire: Boynton/Cook Publishers, 1988.

Highlights the use of peer response in writing classes in a detailed and comprehensive manner.

Torbe, Mike and Medway, Peter. *The Climate for Learning*. London: Ward Lock Educational, 1981.

A comprehensive account of learning through language across the curriculum.